Creative Hope

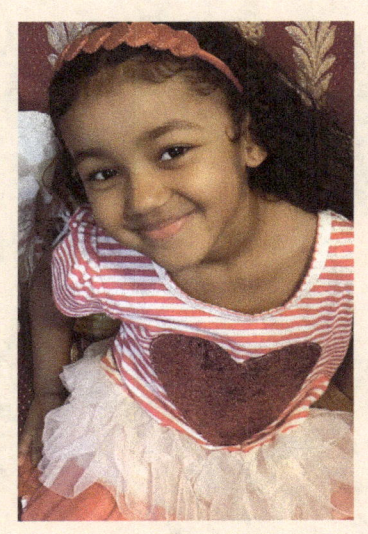

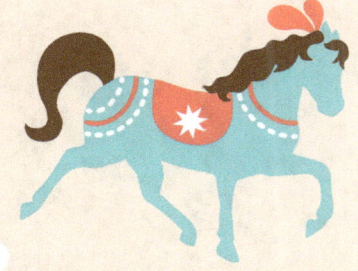

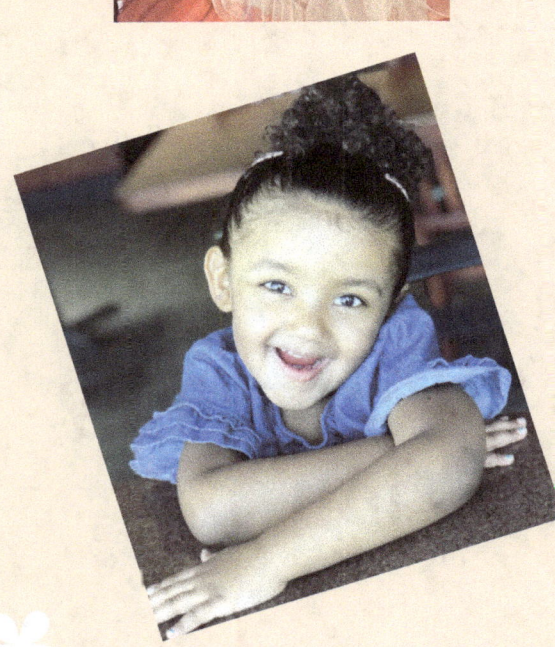

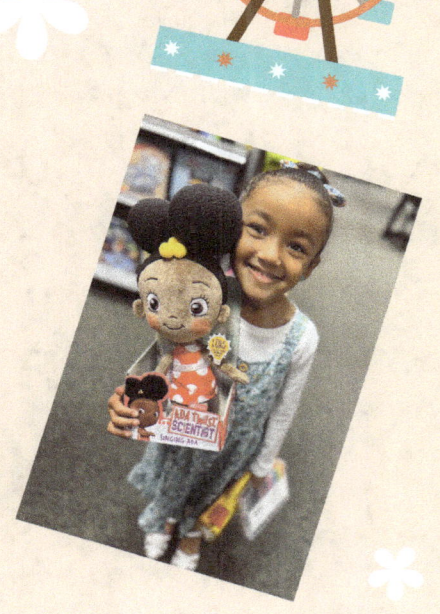

WRITTEN & ILLUSTRATION
BY HOPE ZION

Creative Hope

Written & Ilustrated by
Hope Zion

Legal Note

Copyright © by ELIYAHU Shmuel Ben Yah / Hope Batz TZION Perez

DEDICATION

To my G-d YAHWEH, The G-d of Israel.
My mommy Talia, My Daddy Eliyahu, My brother Kaleb
Levi. Grandma Aida Rivera , Tio Jose Rivera, Titi Jessica Rivera.
Special Thanks to Min.Donna Lynn & Walter Austin, Min. Sheila Morgan,
Miriam Rodriguez, Josue Rodriguez (David Shmuel Ben Zion)

My Special Friends: ELIJAH SMITH & JEREMIAH

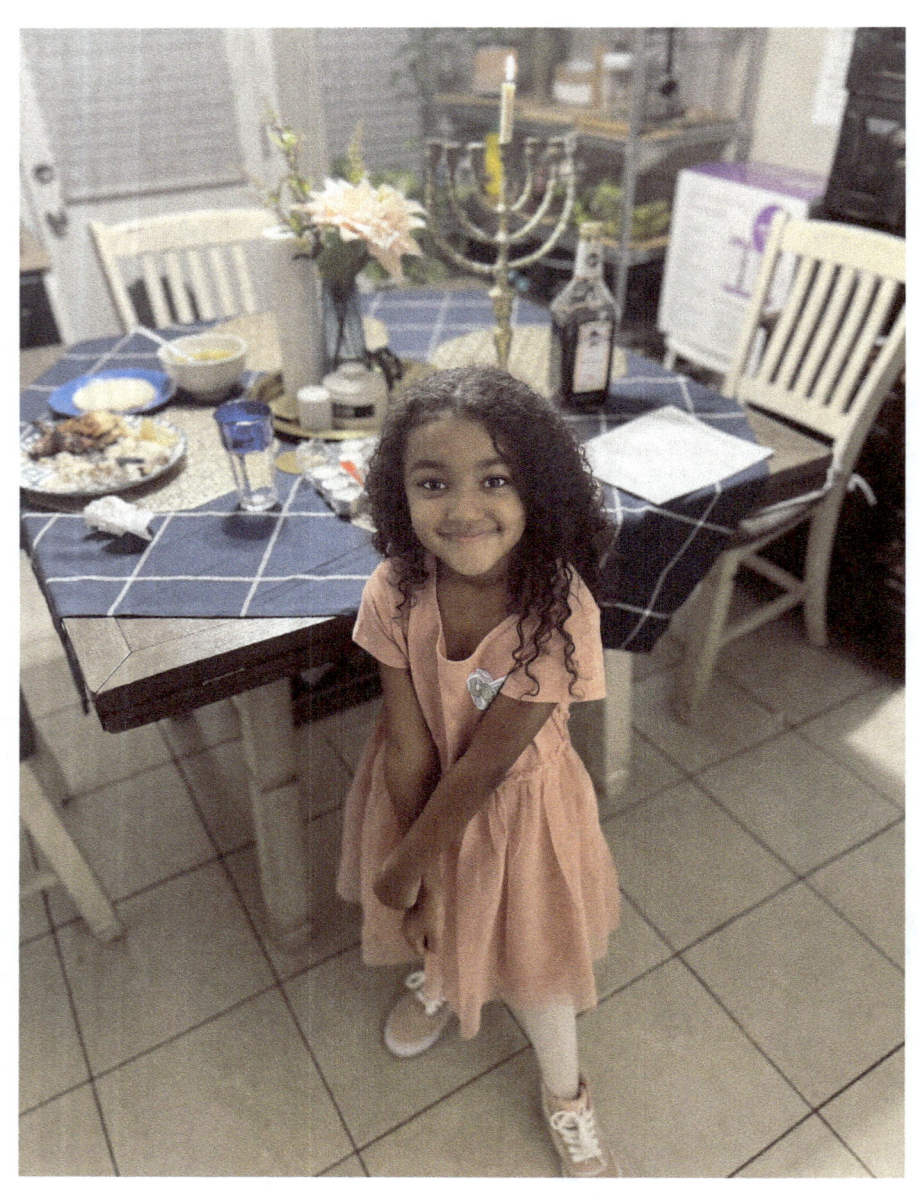

Celebrating my 7th Year of Hanukkah

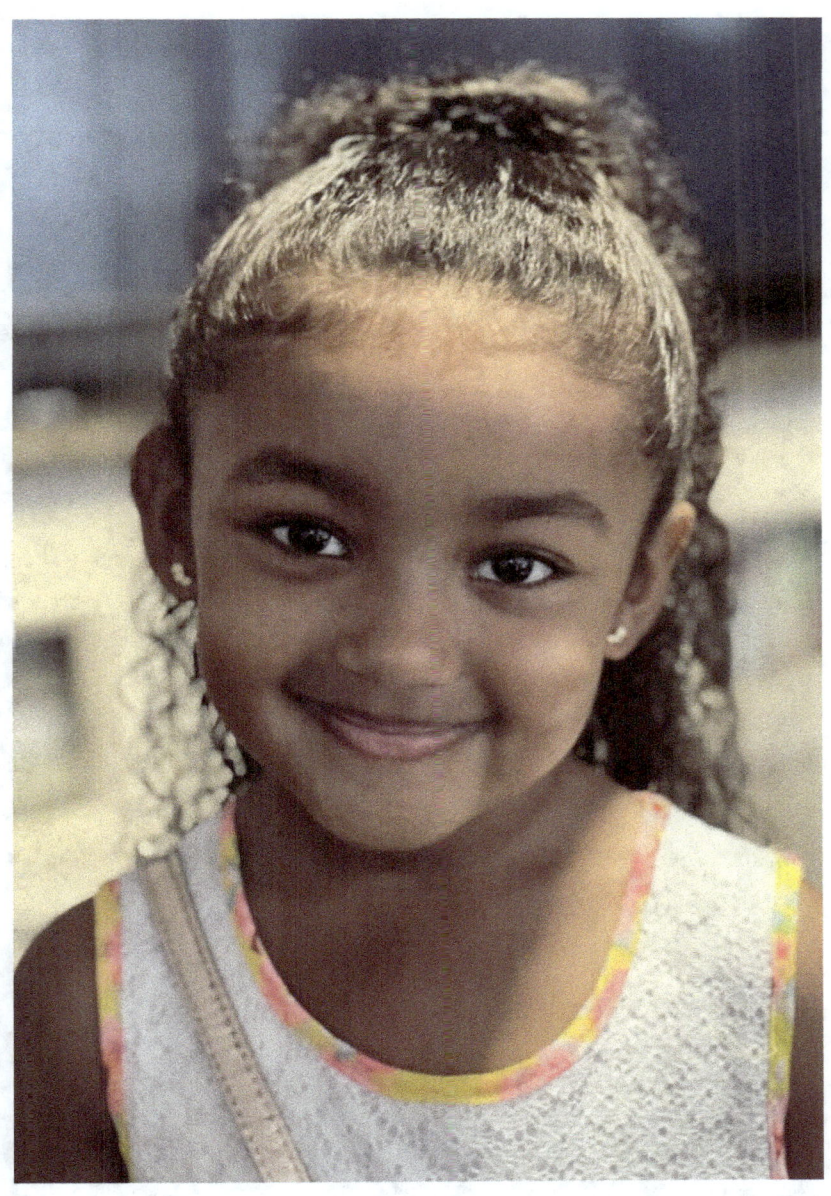

Heaven Hi, my name is Hope Zion, I'm currently 7 Years old. I drew all these pictures using my imagination. My Daddy asked if I wanted my own picture book and I said: "YES!" I hope you ENJOY! Ooooh, did I forget to mention that I'm an honorary chaplain? This is my birthday gift August 28th 2023. My Daady promised to publish my artwork and turn into a book and so here it is!

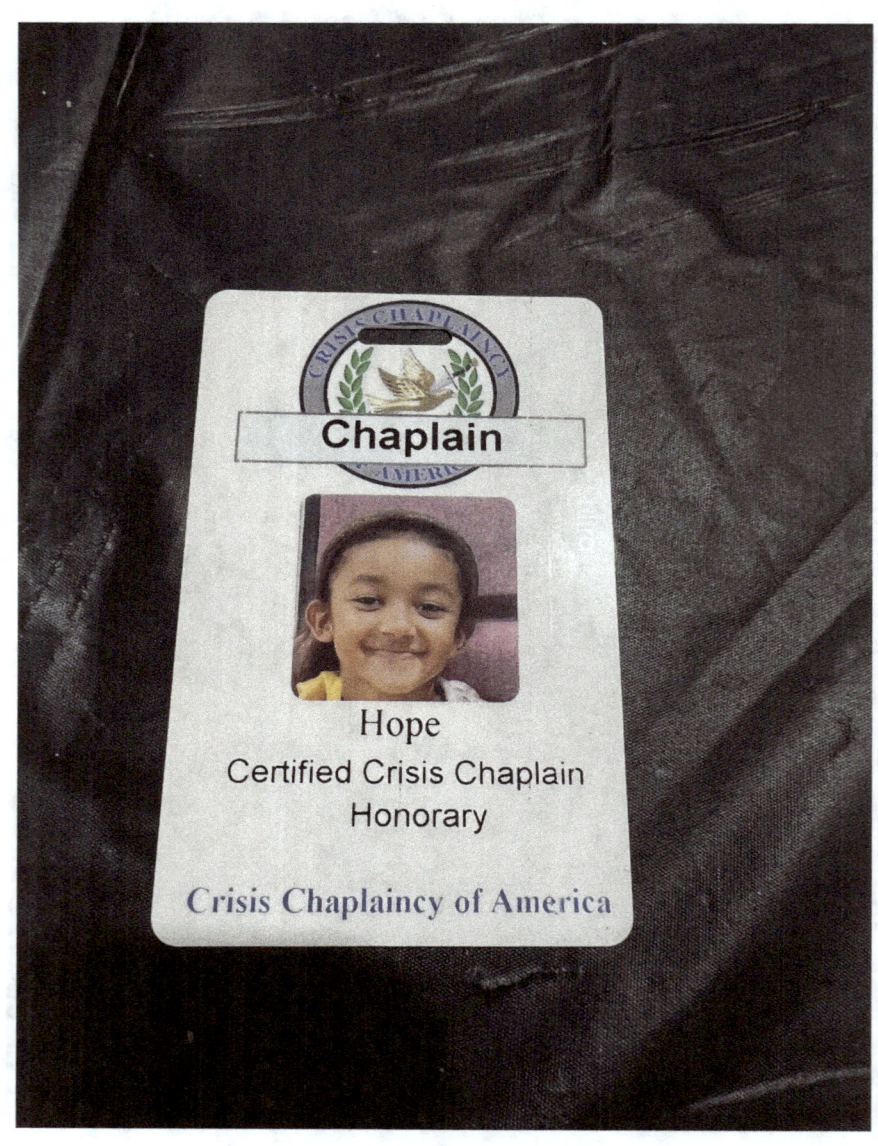

I told you! I'm an Honorary Chaplain with my mommy and daddy

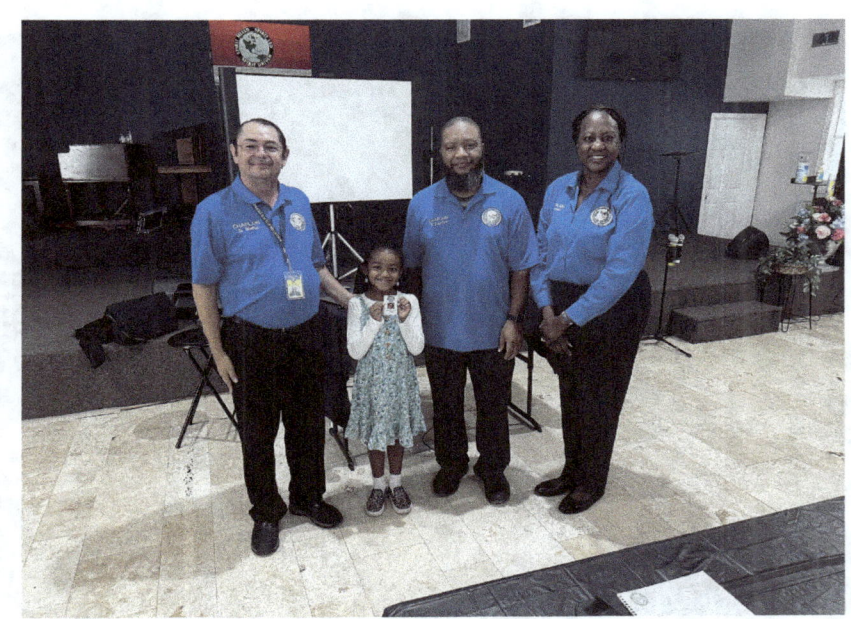

My Teacher Lunetta Mitchell

The Graduating class of chaplains, Oct. 21, 2023

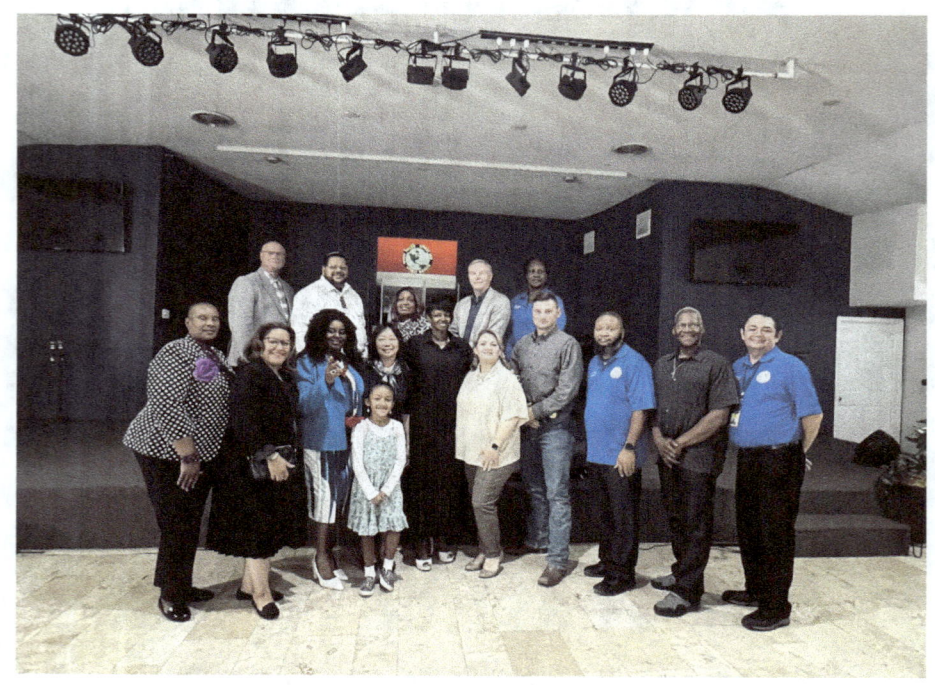

See! I'm in the middle, the little one.

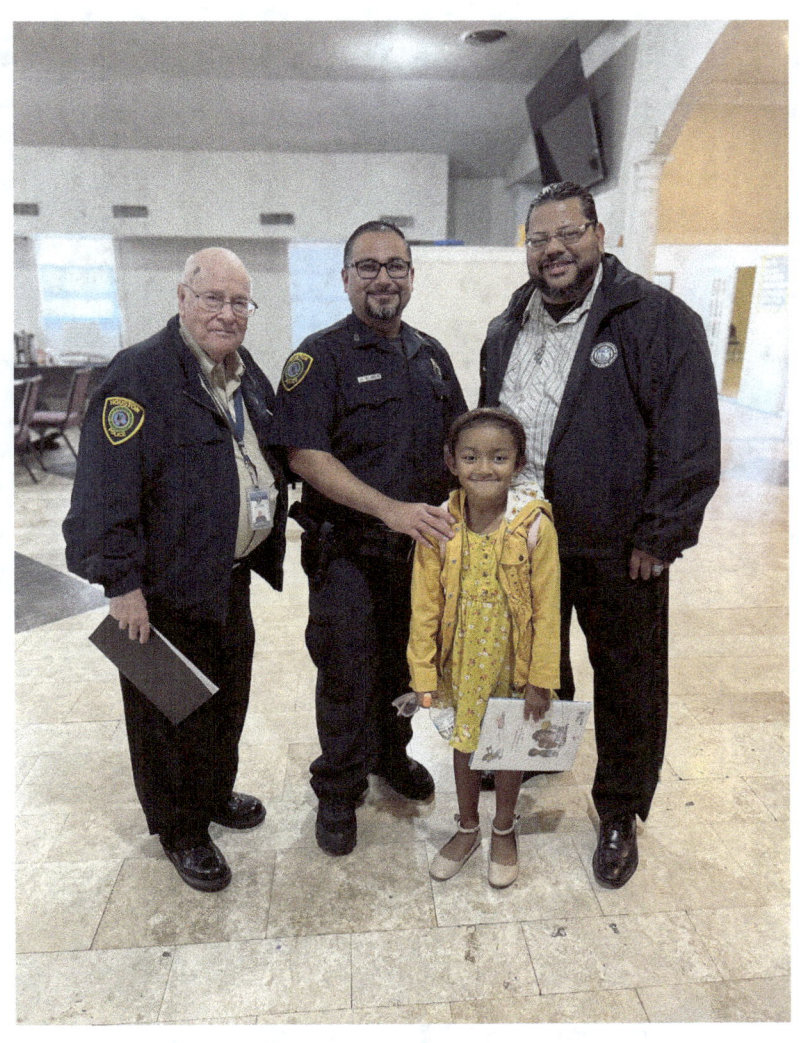

I'm here with my daddy, Mr. Eddie Hestand and Officer/ Chaplain Julio Villareal. HPD (Houston Police)

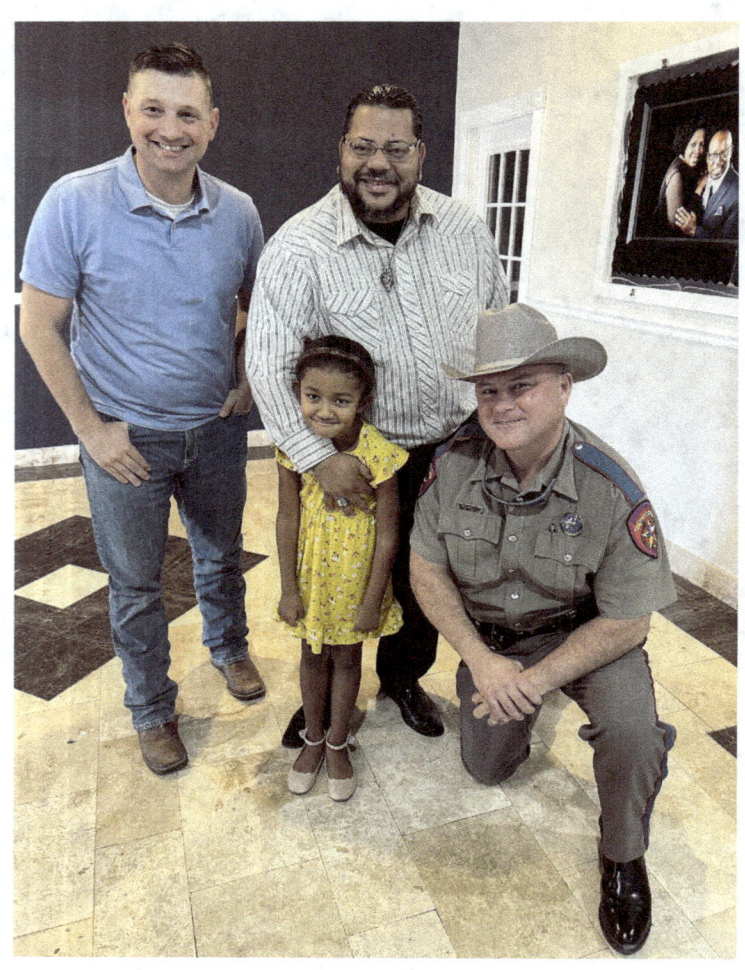

Wohooo! My daddy sure
loves to take pictures.
These two men are
Texas State Troopers.

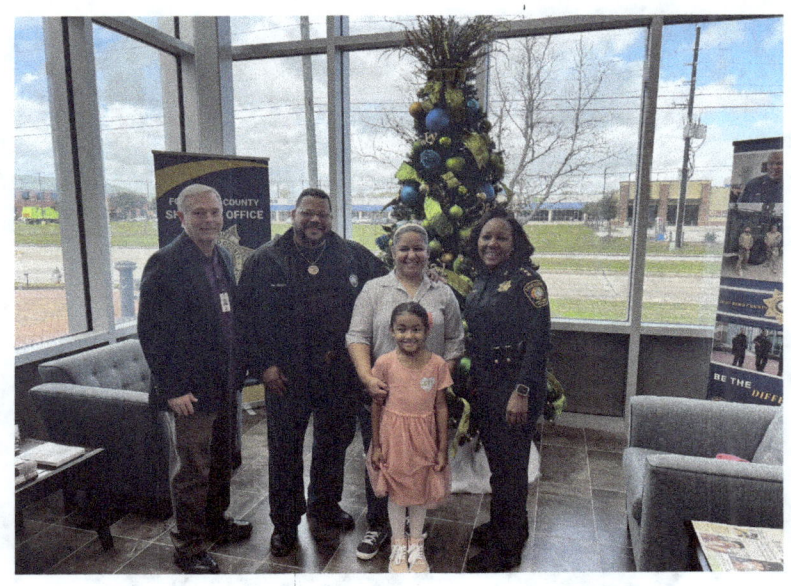

That's me in the middle!
Im with my daddy, Mommy, Deputy Sheriff Barry Curtis and Chief Sheriff Mattie C. Provost. My mommy and daddy are Chaplains for the Fort end Sheriff (Volunteer)

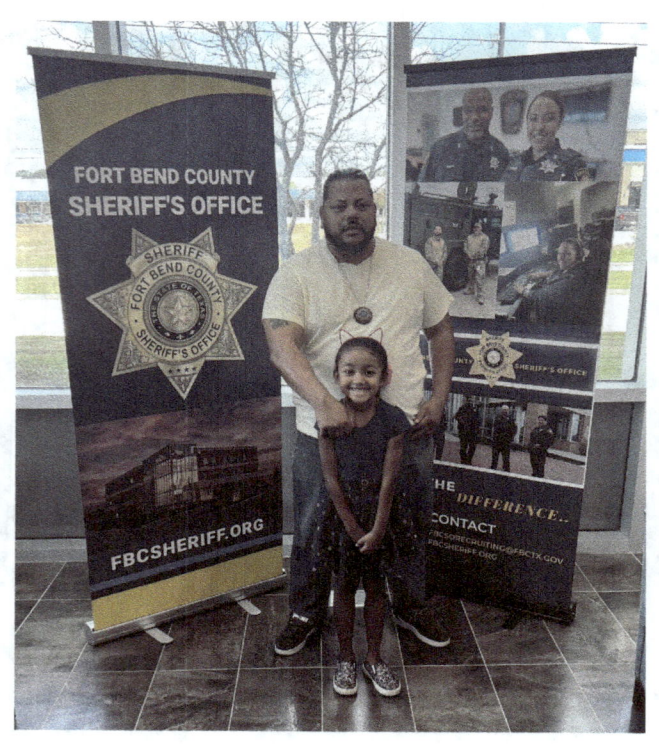

Me and my daddy.

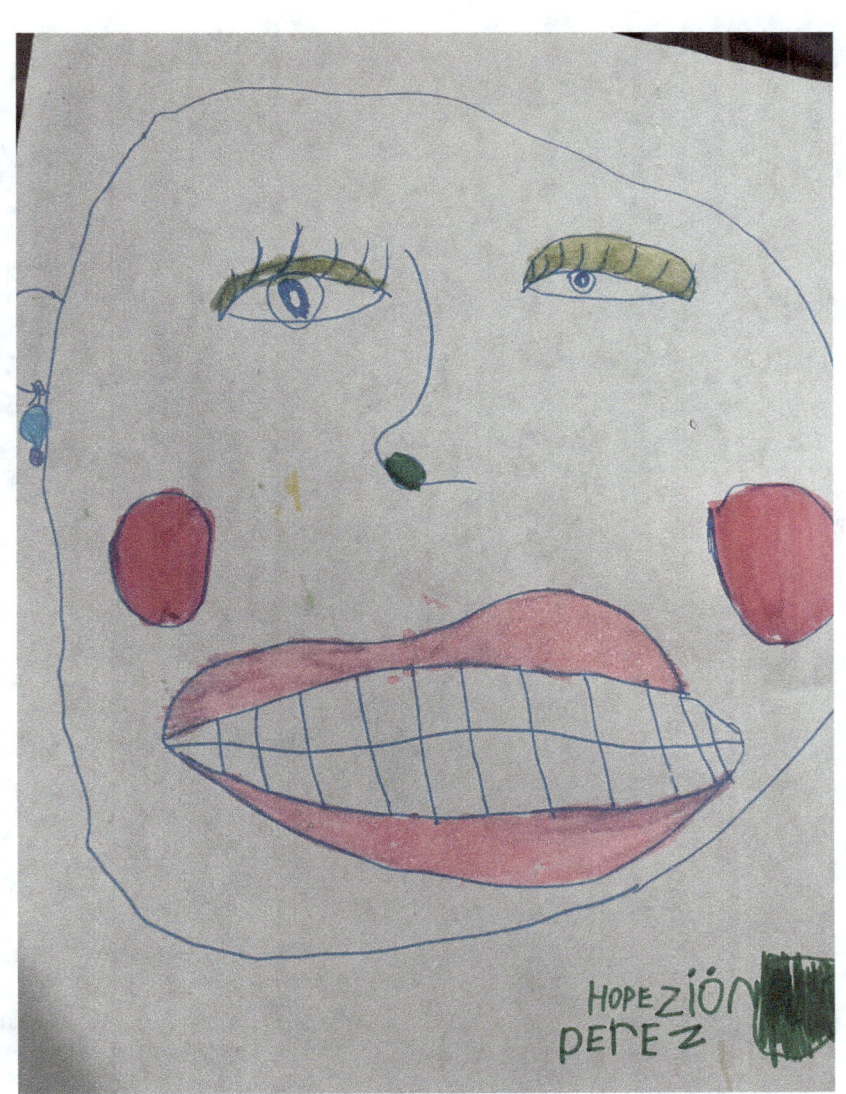

HOPE ZION
PEREZ

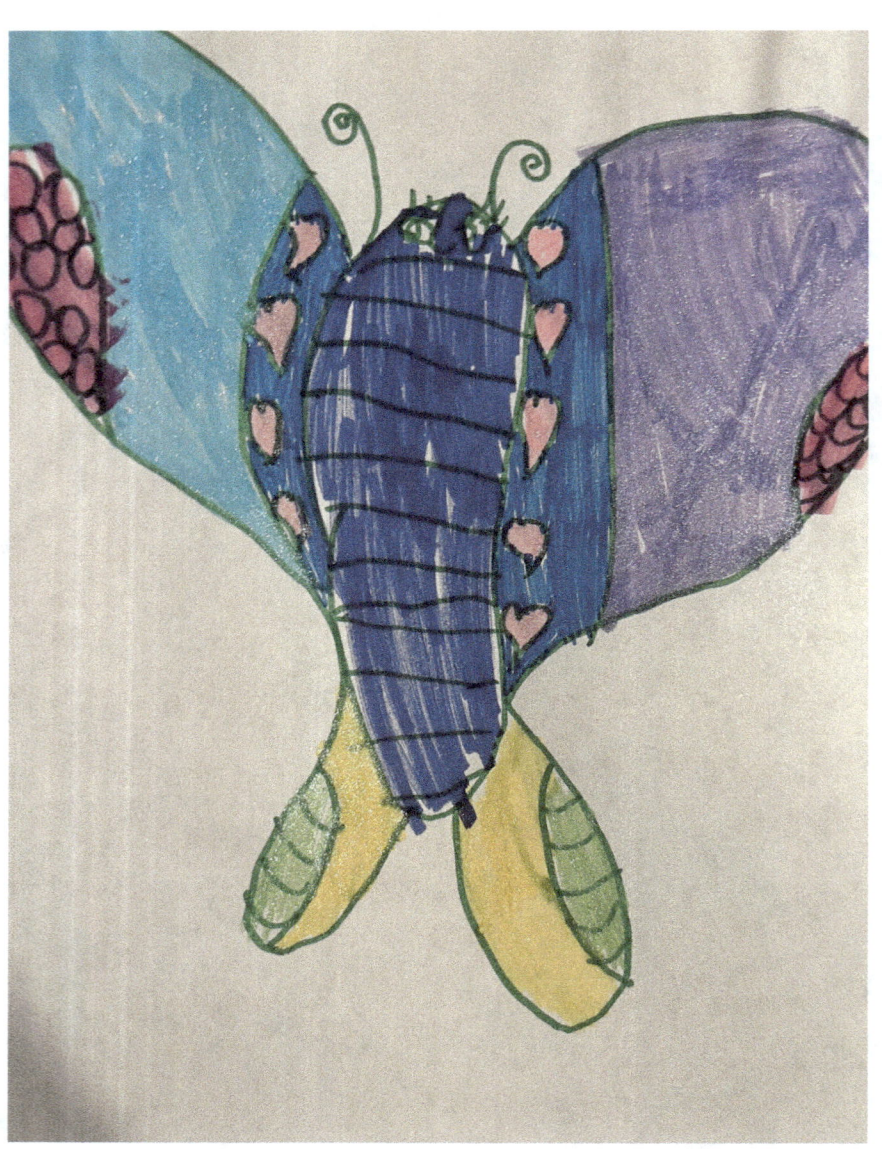

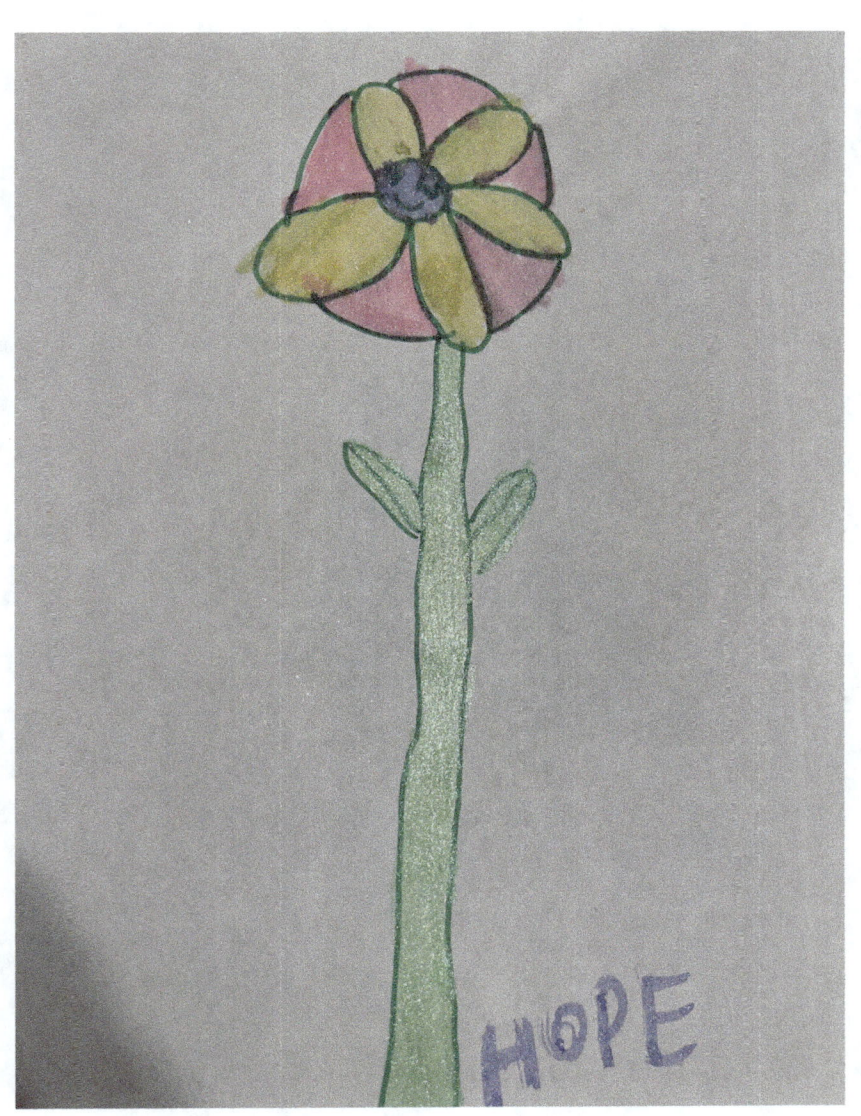

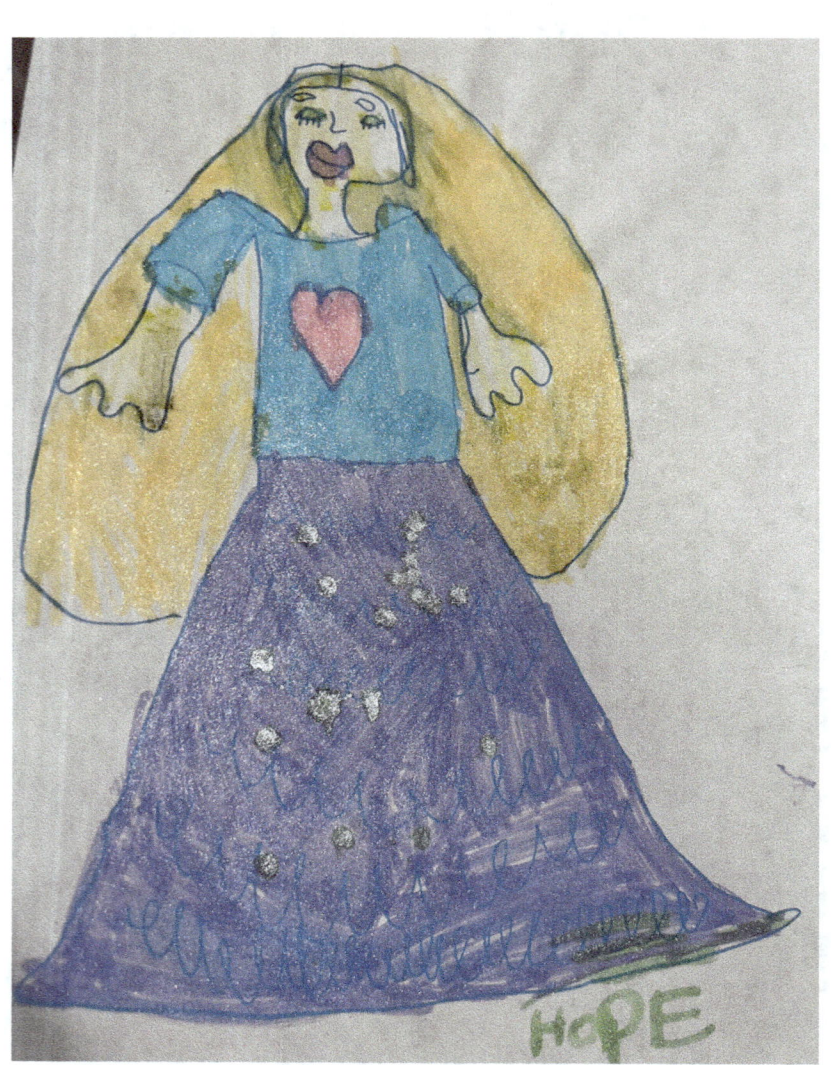

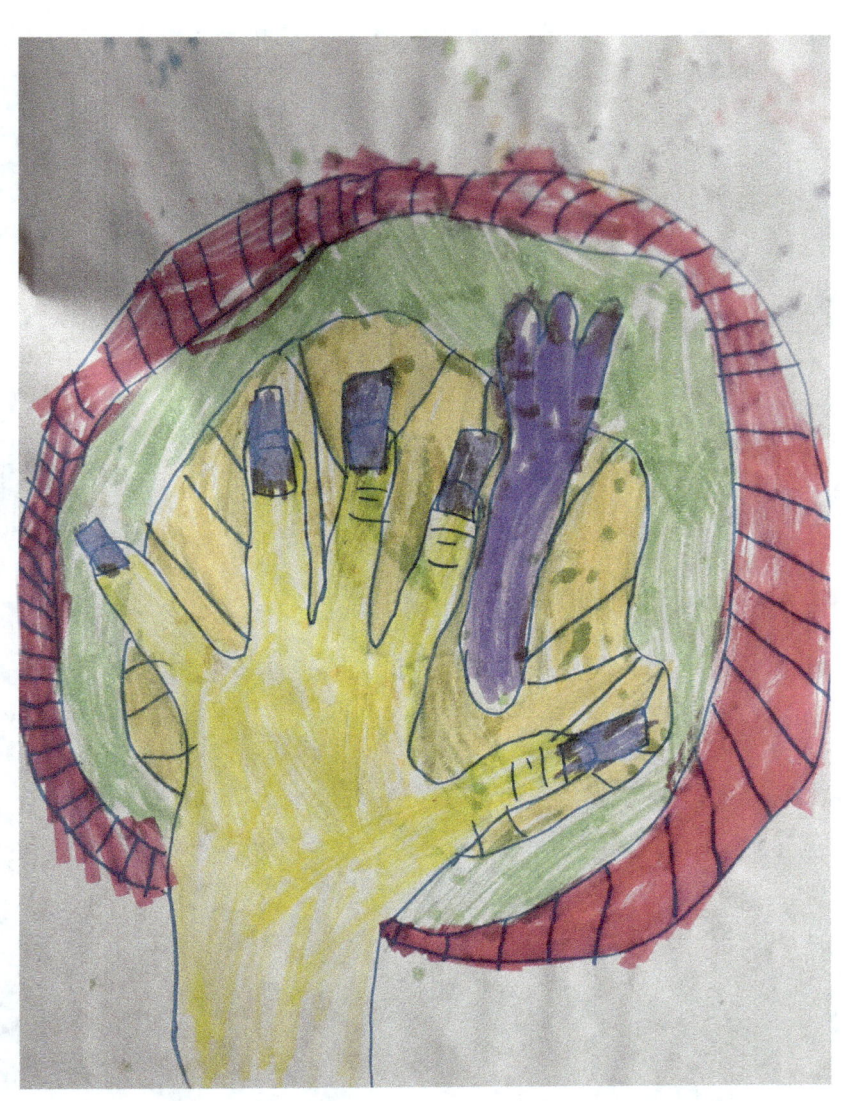

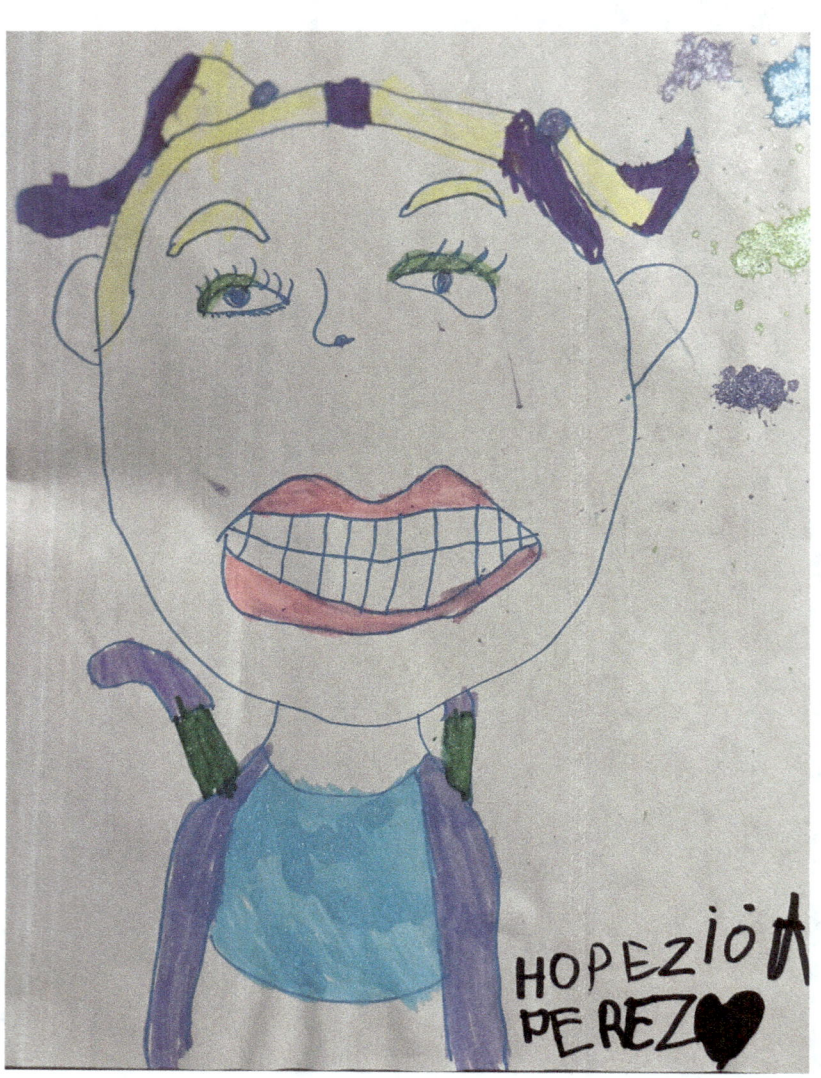

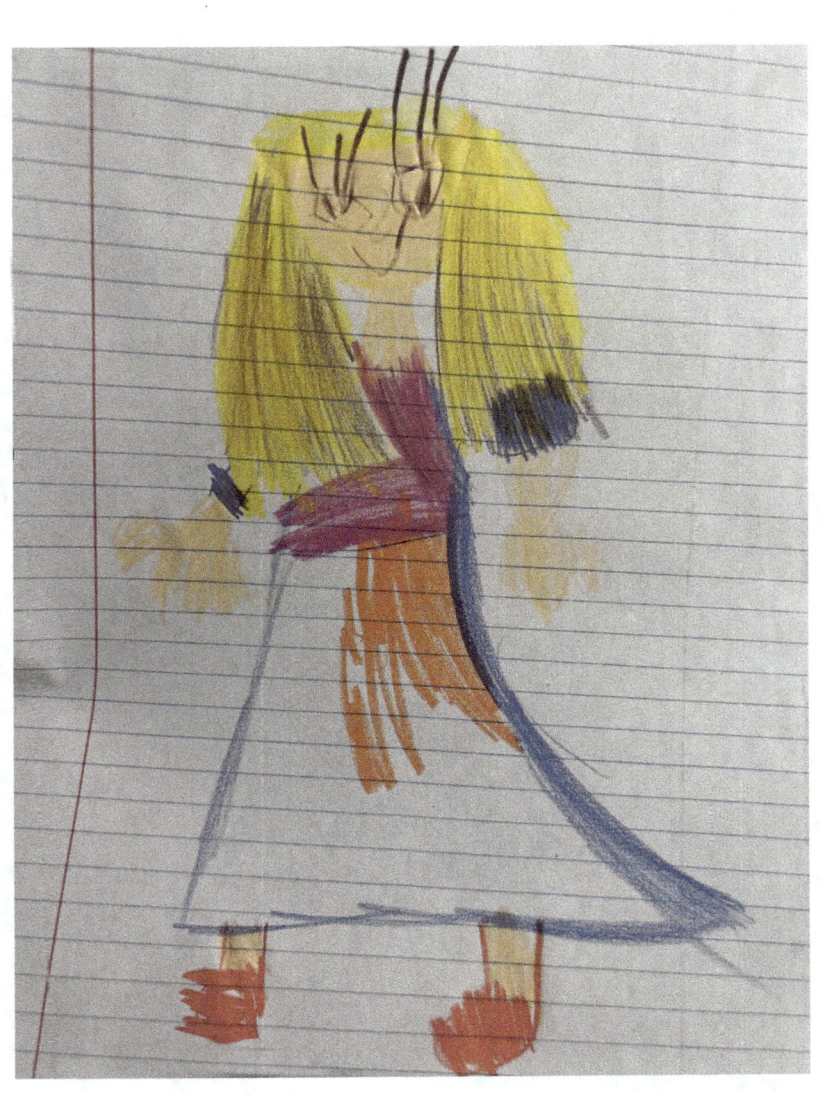

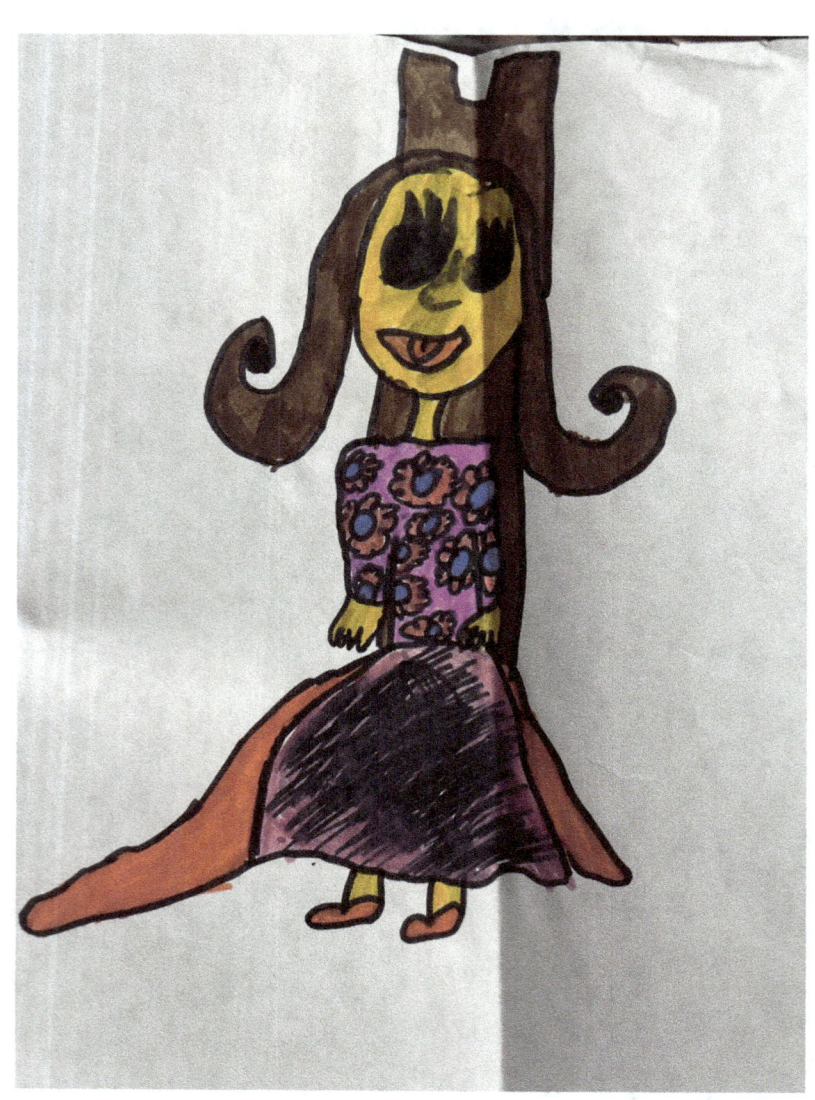

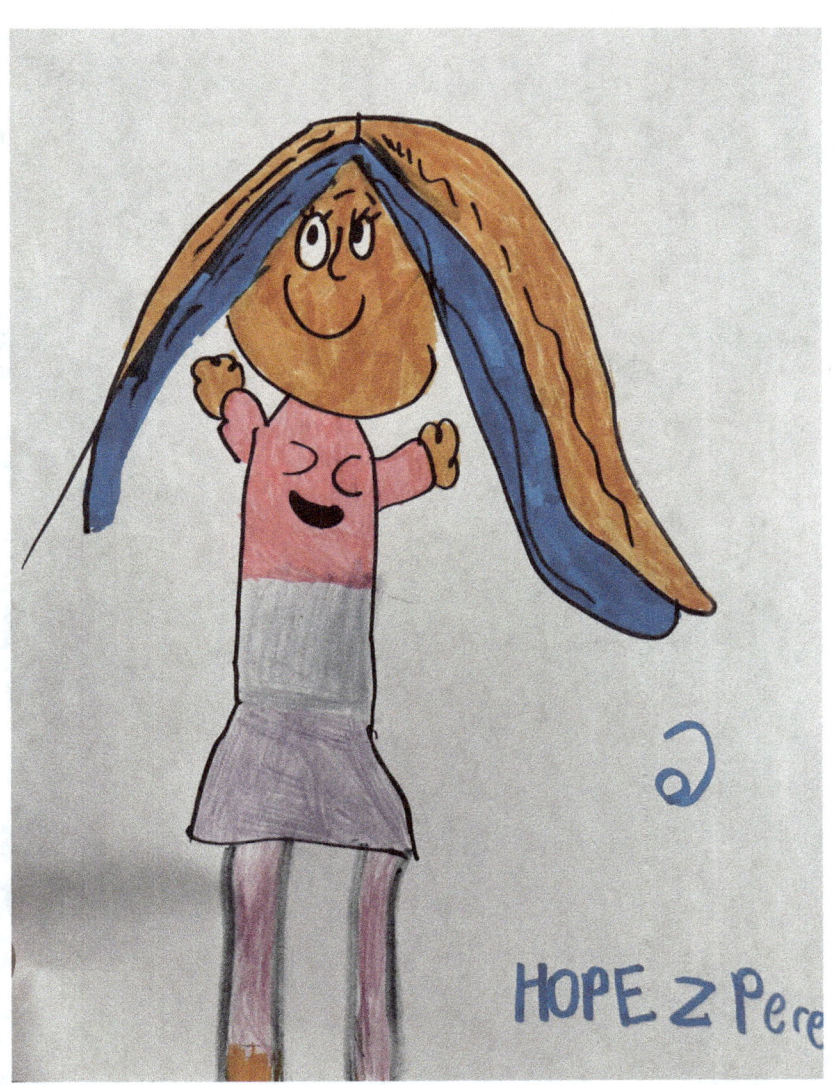

HOPE z Pere

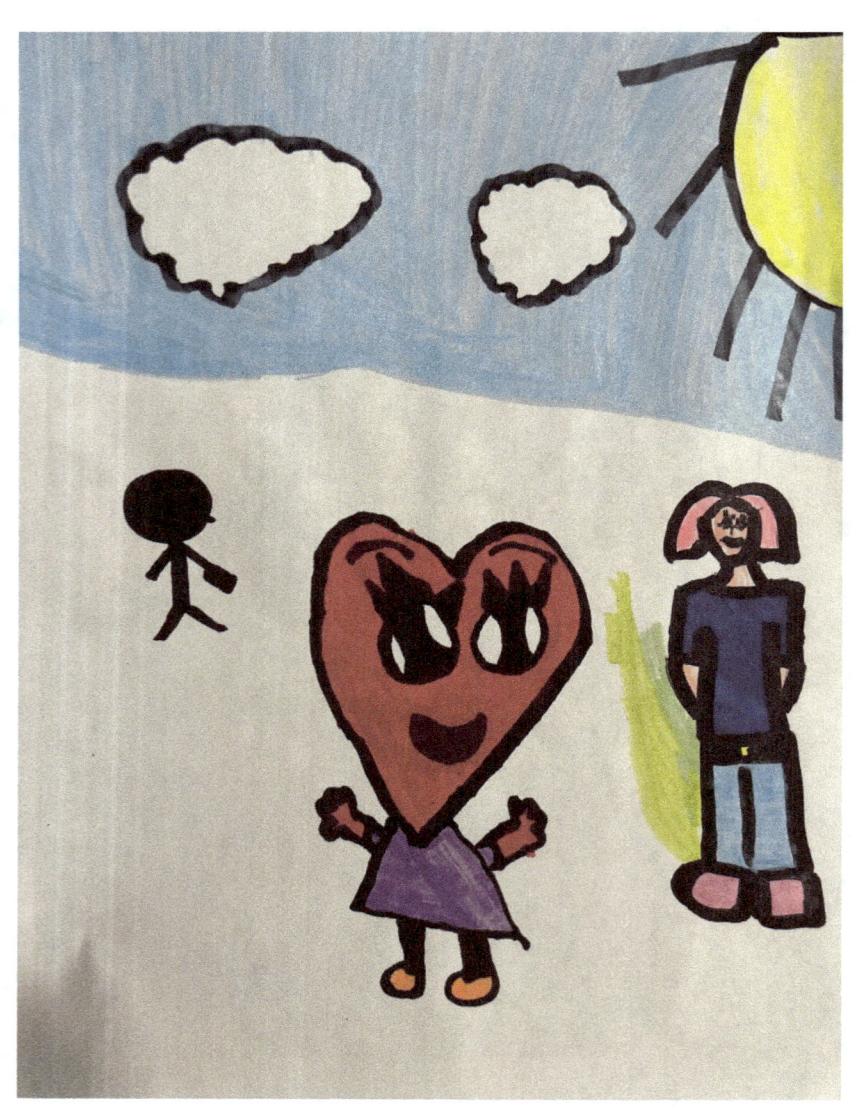

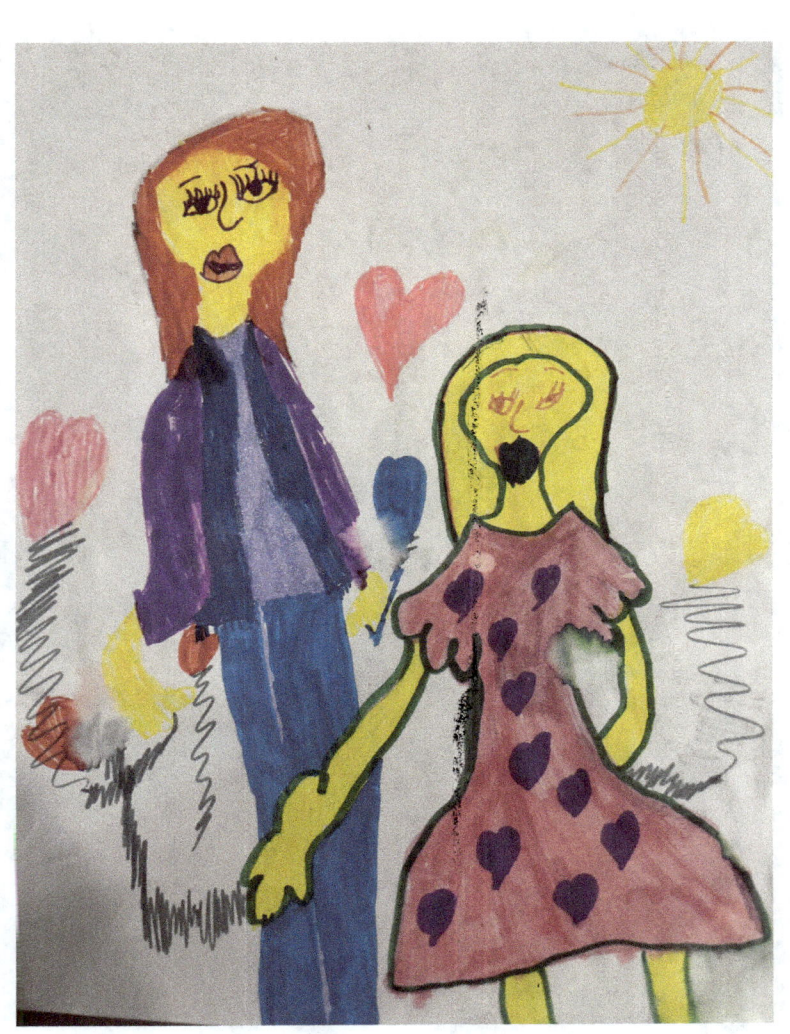

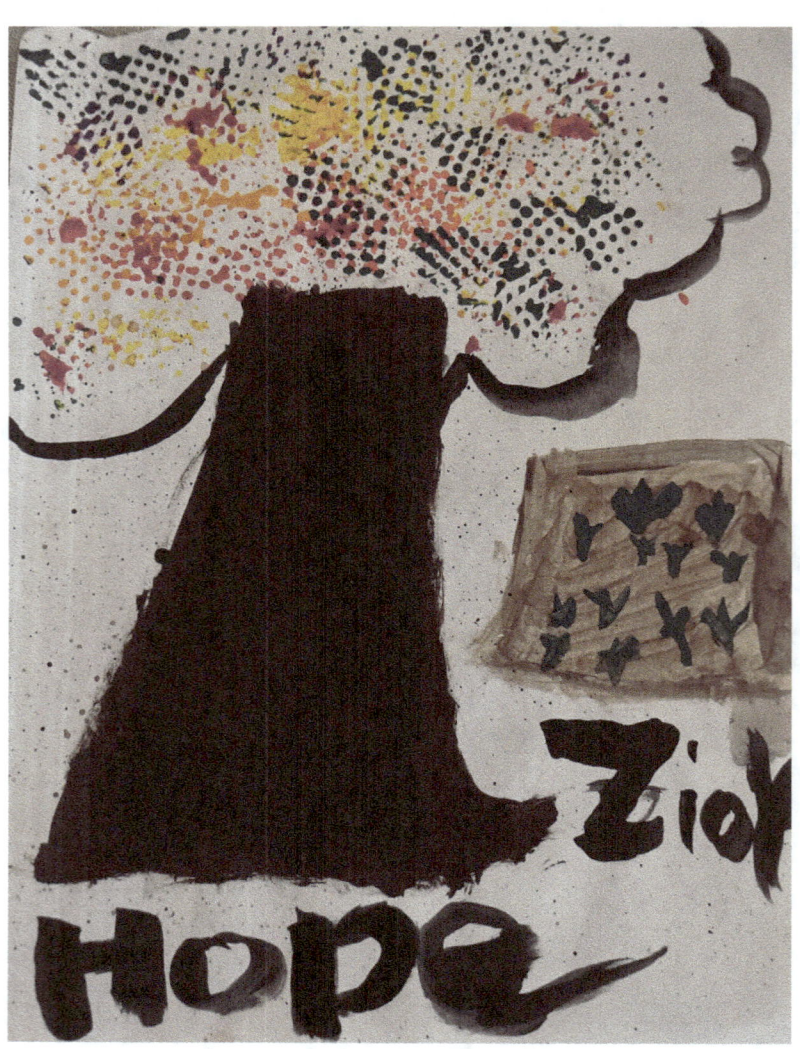

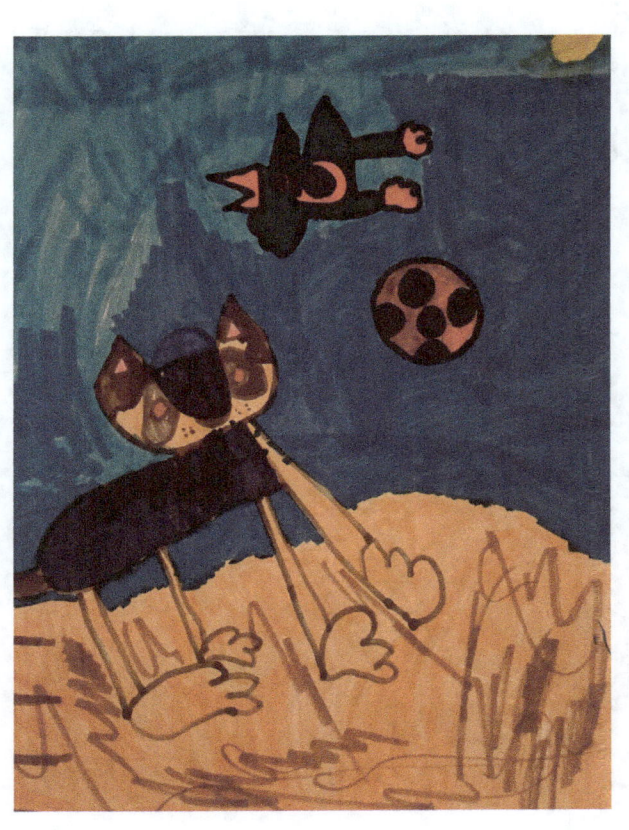

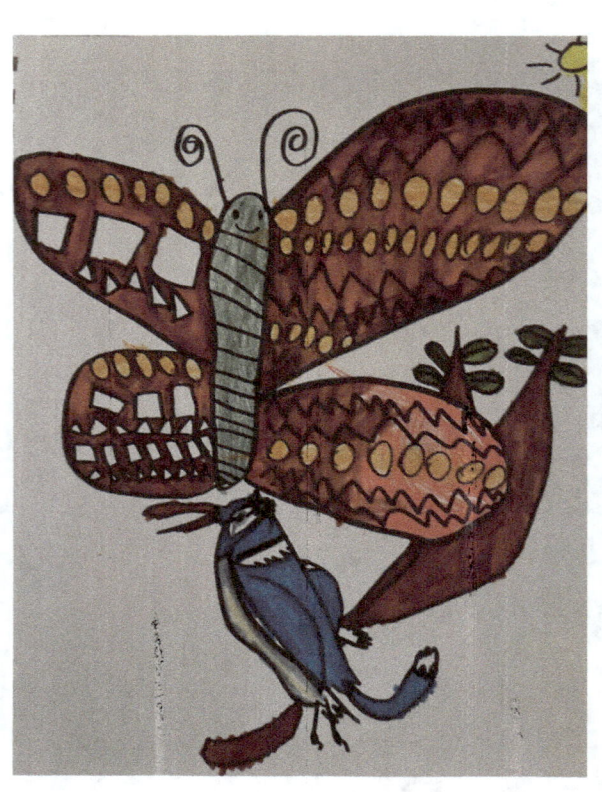

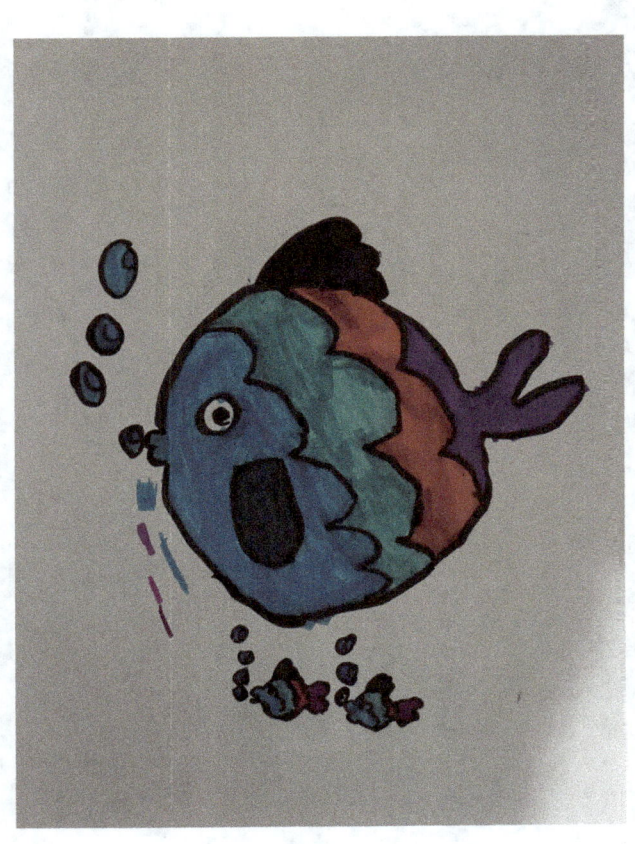

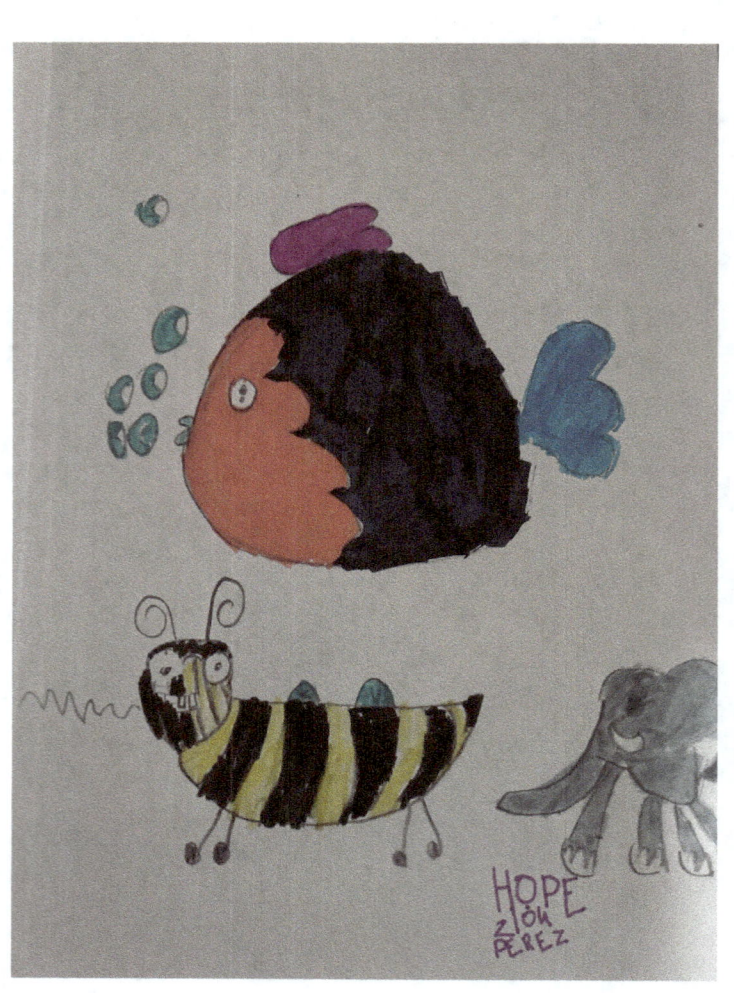

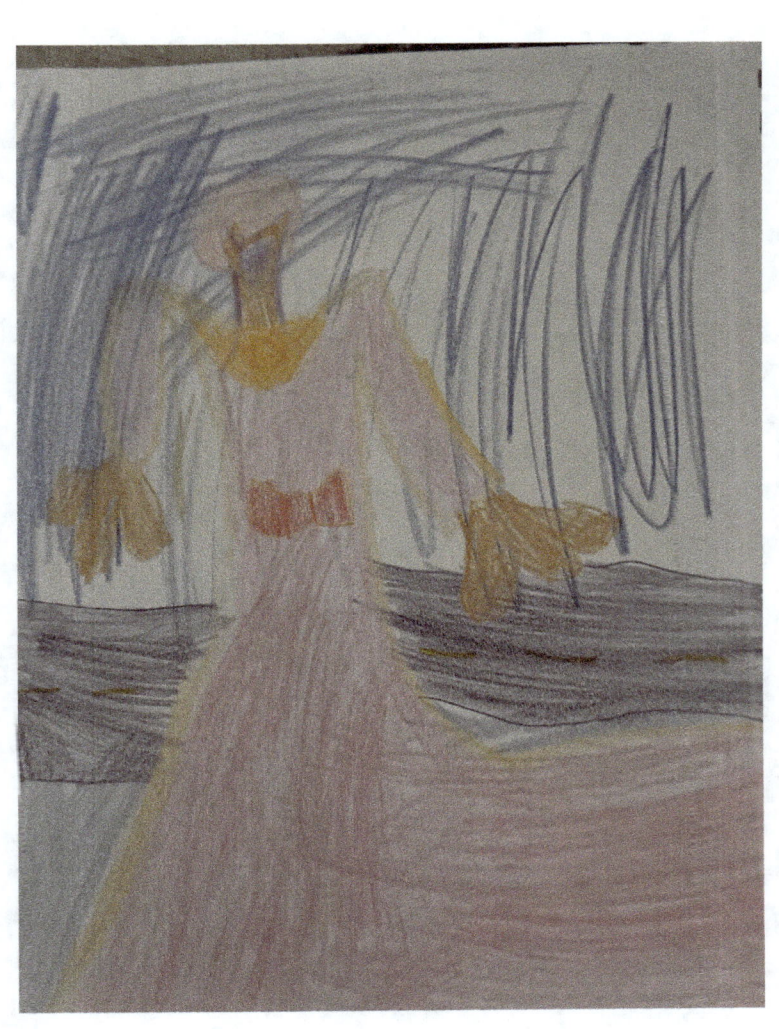

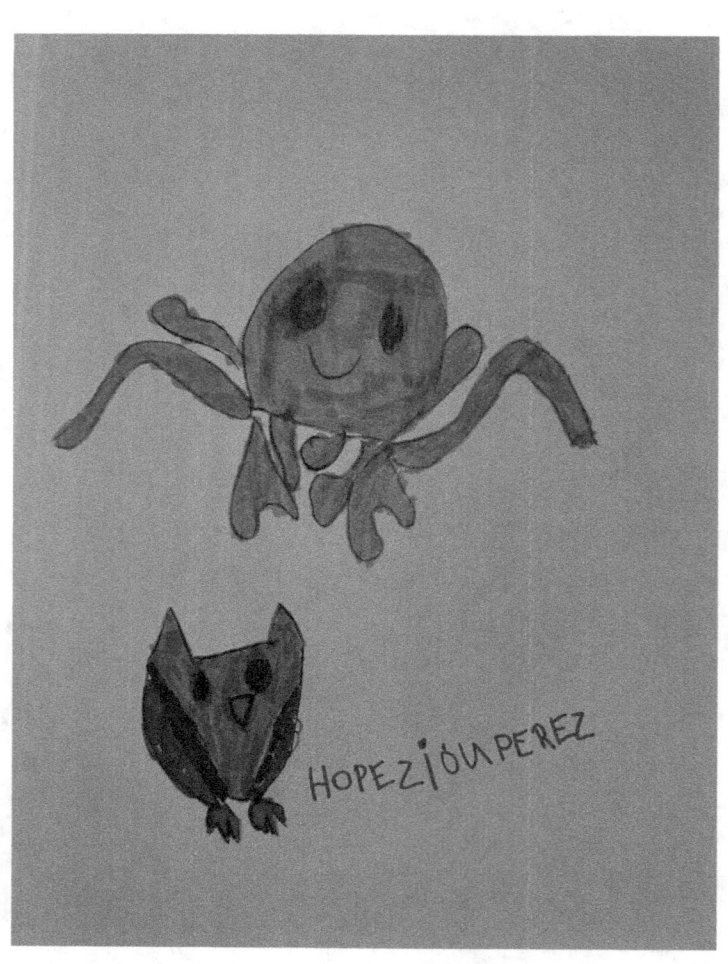

HOPEZiou PEREZ

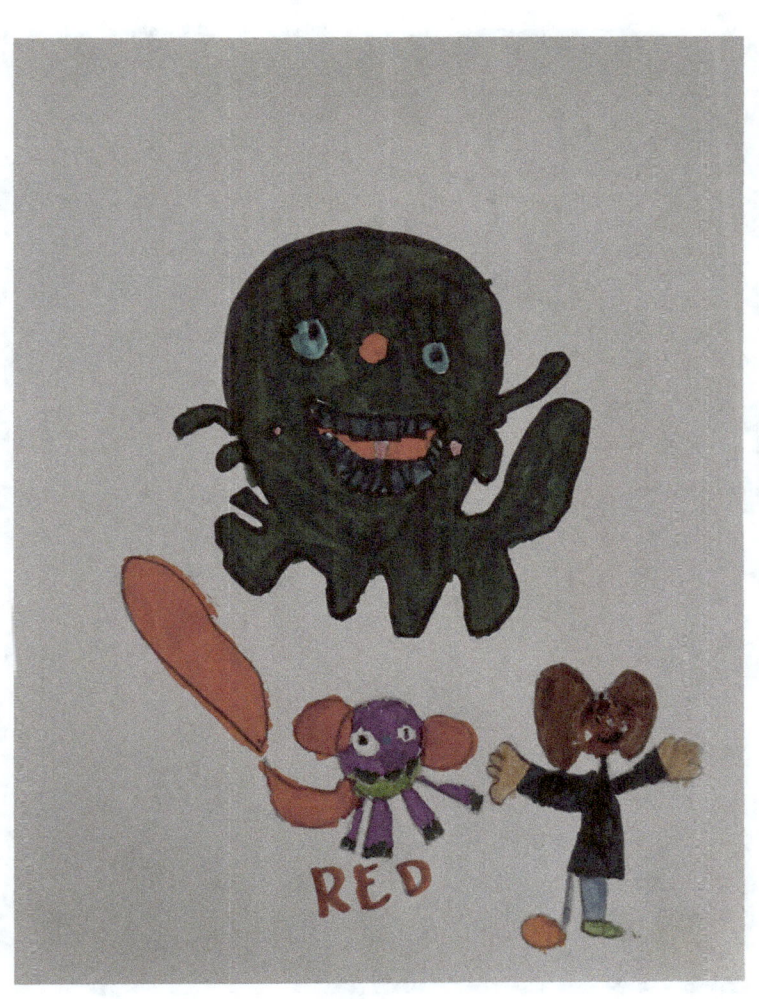

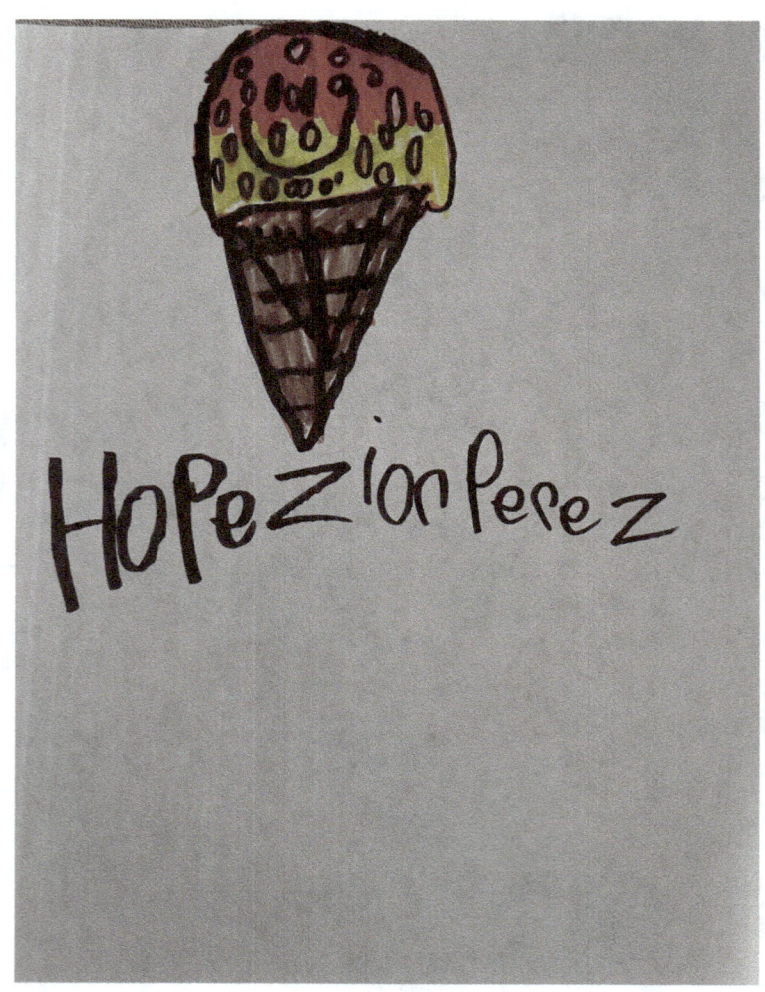

HOPeZionPerez

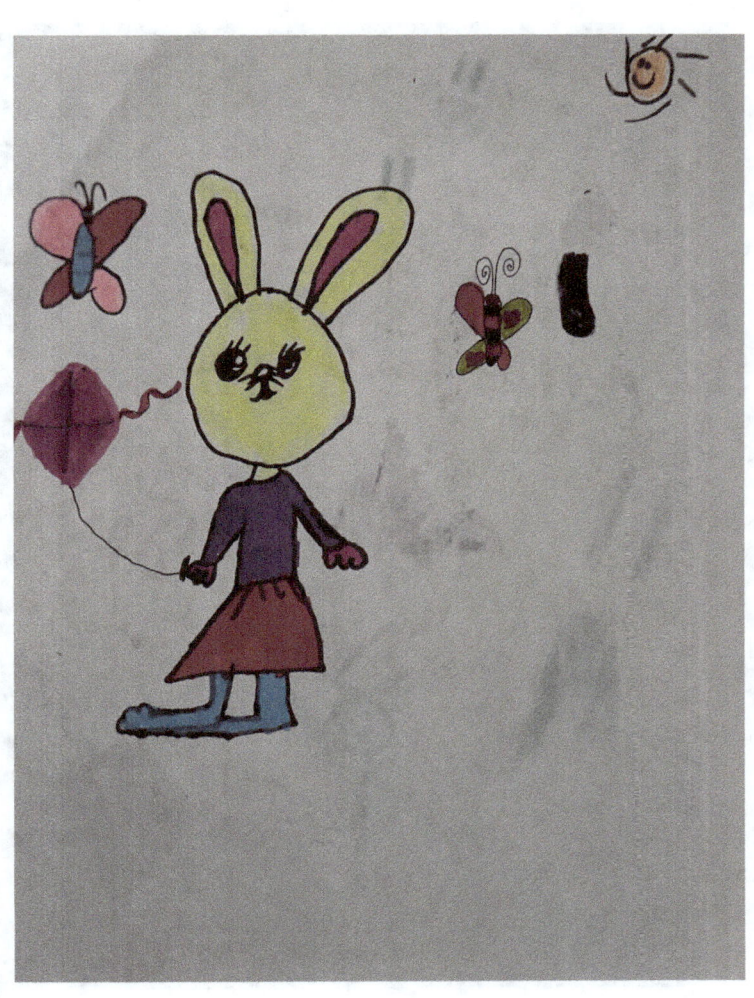

My plate is full of _Thanks_ .

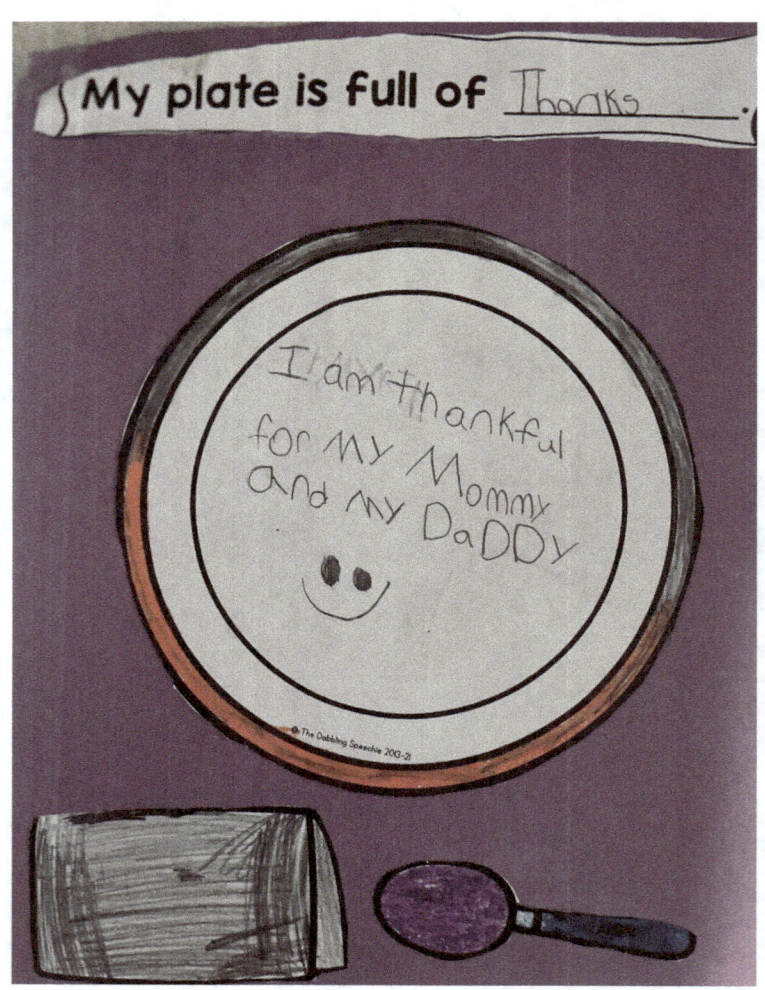

I am thankful
for my Mommy
and my DaDDY

© The Dabbling Speechie 2010-21

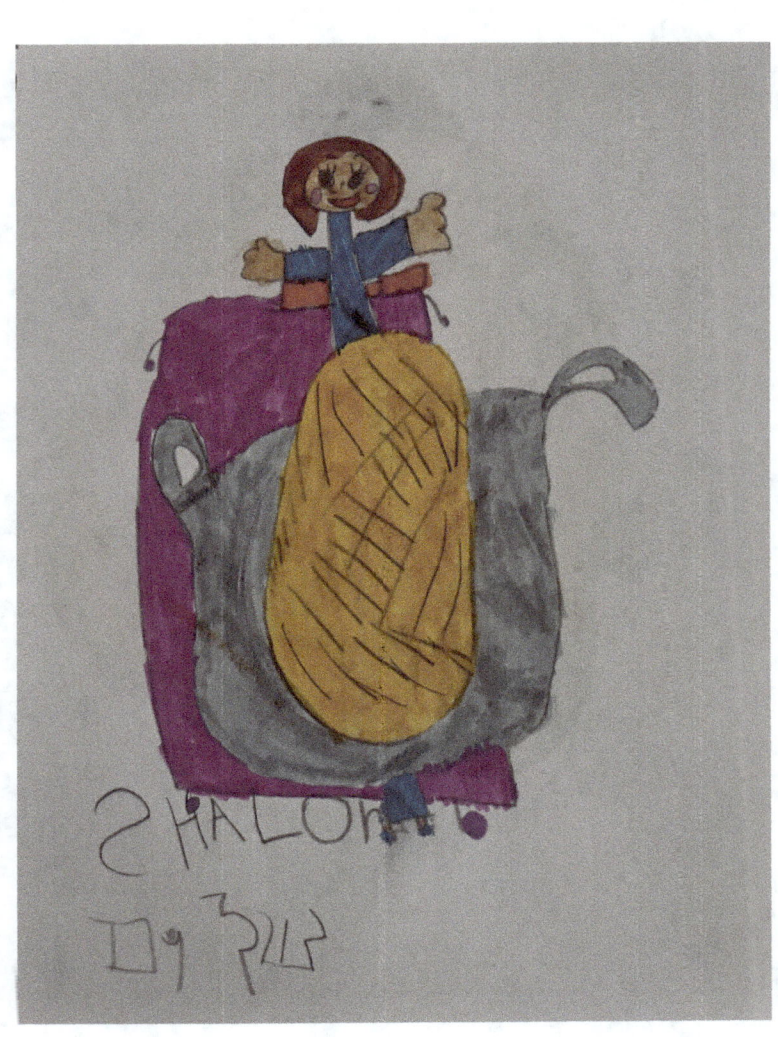

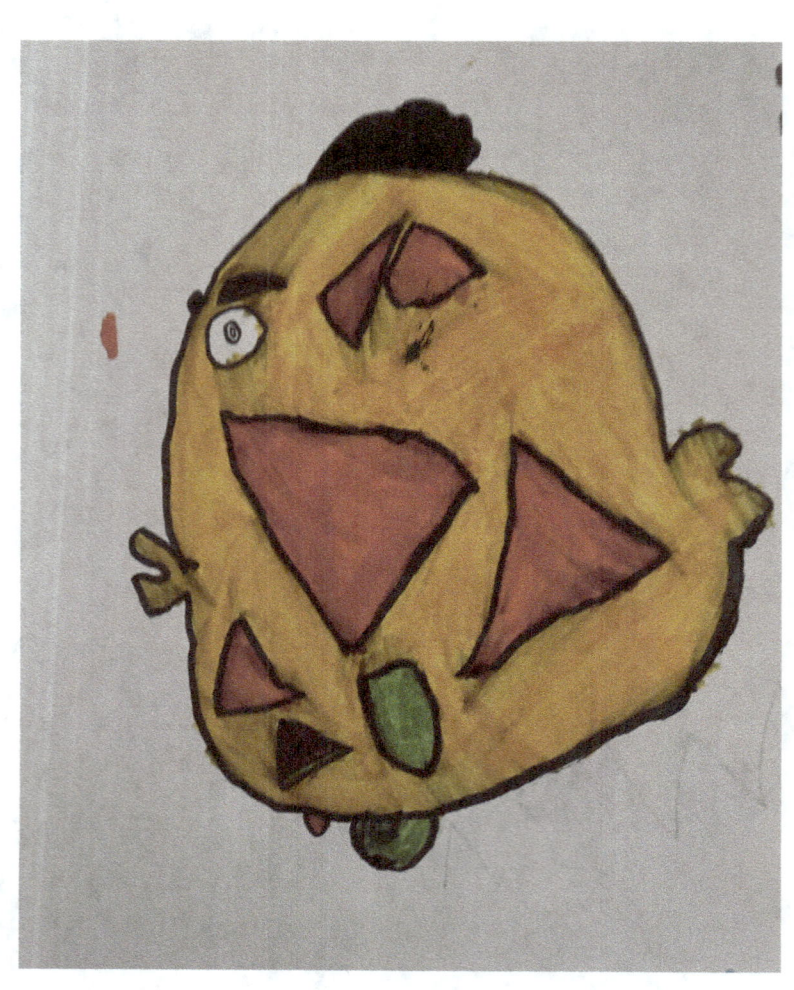

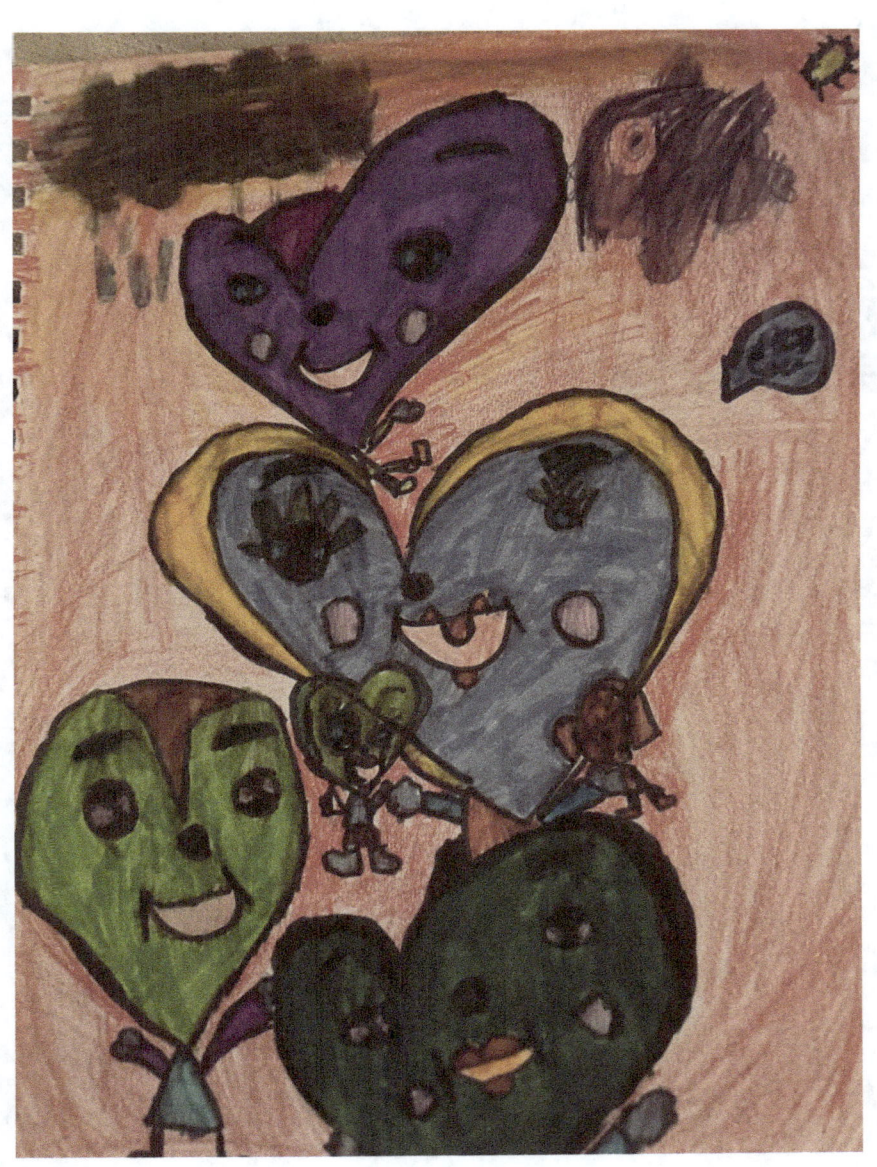

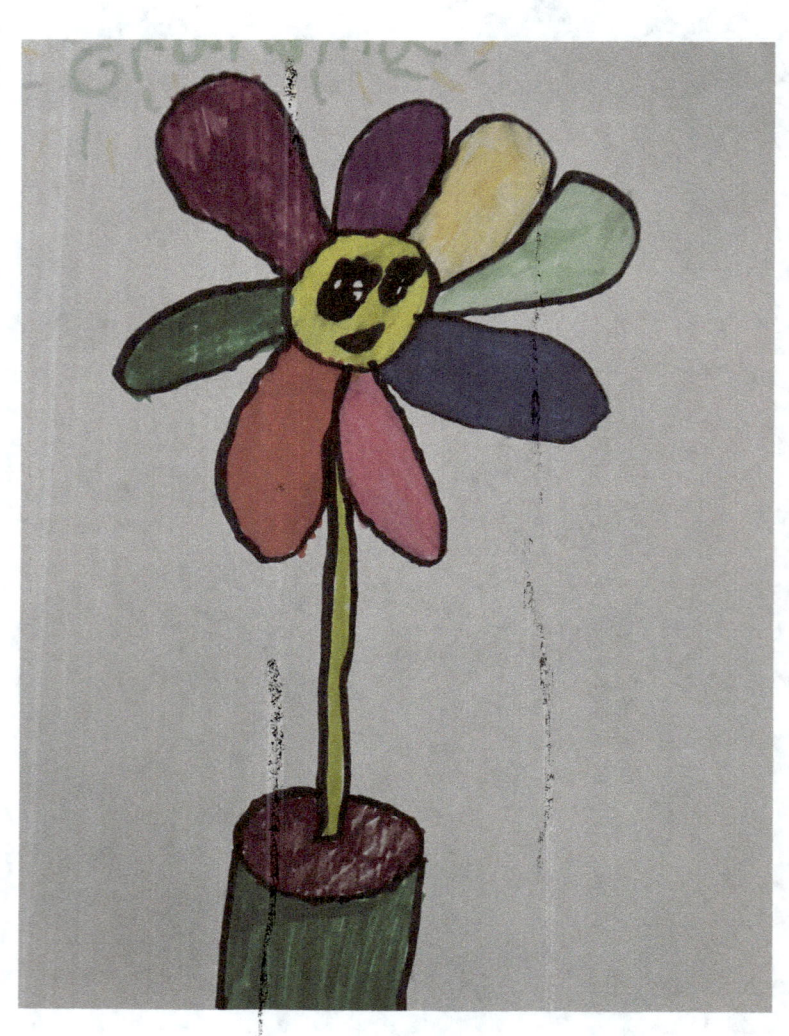

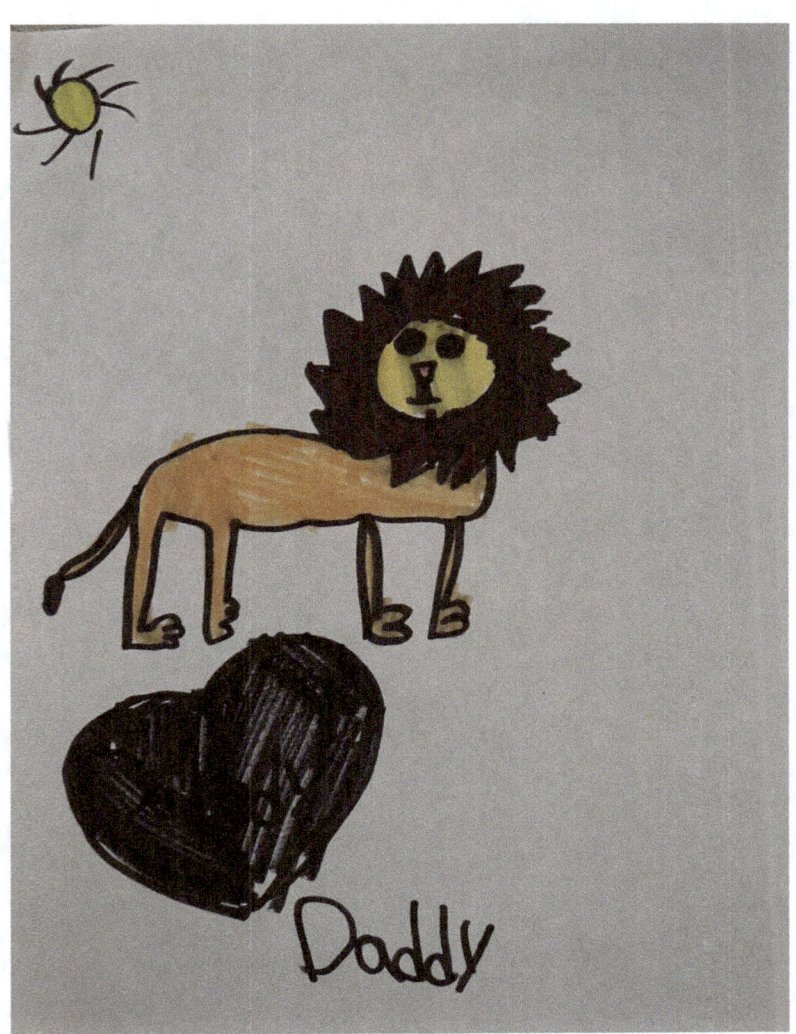

Daddy

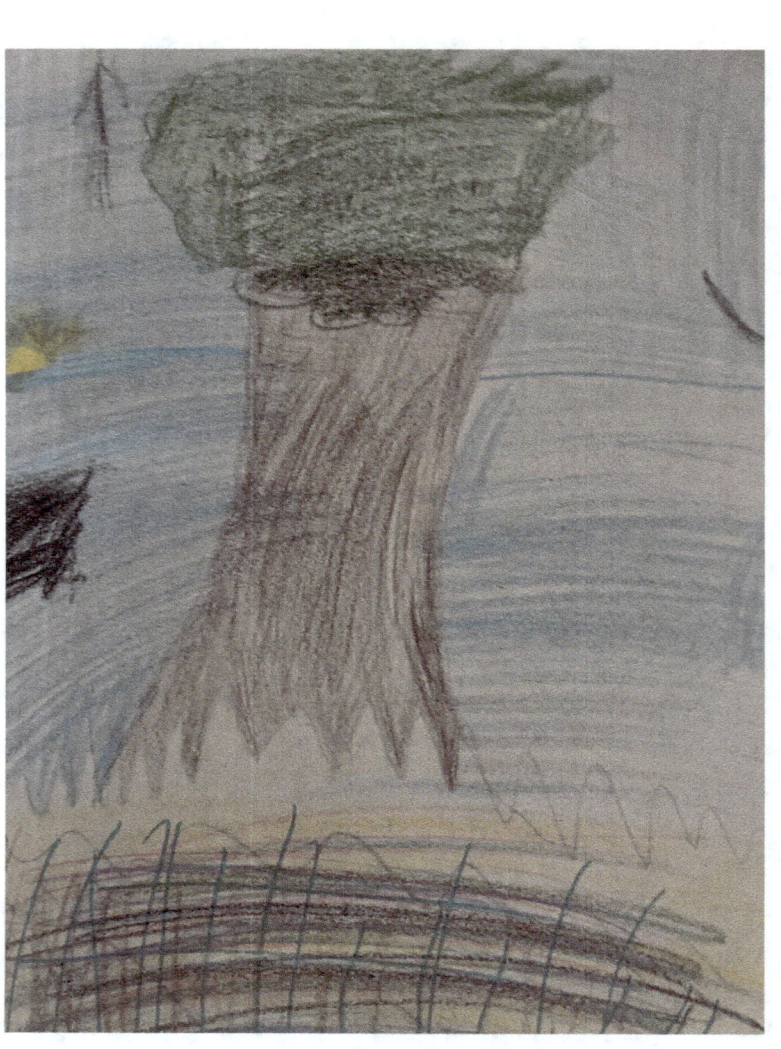

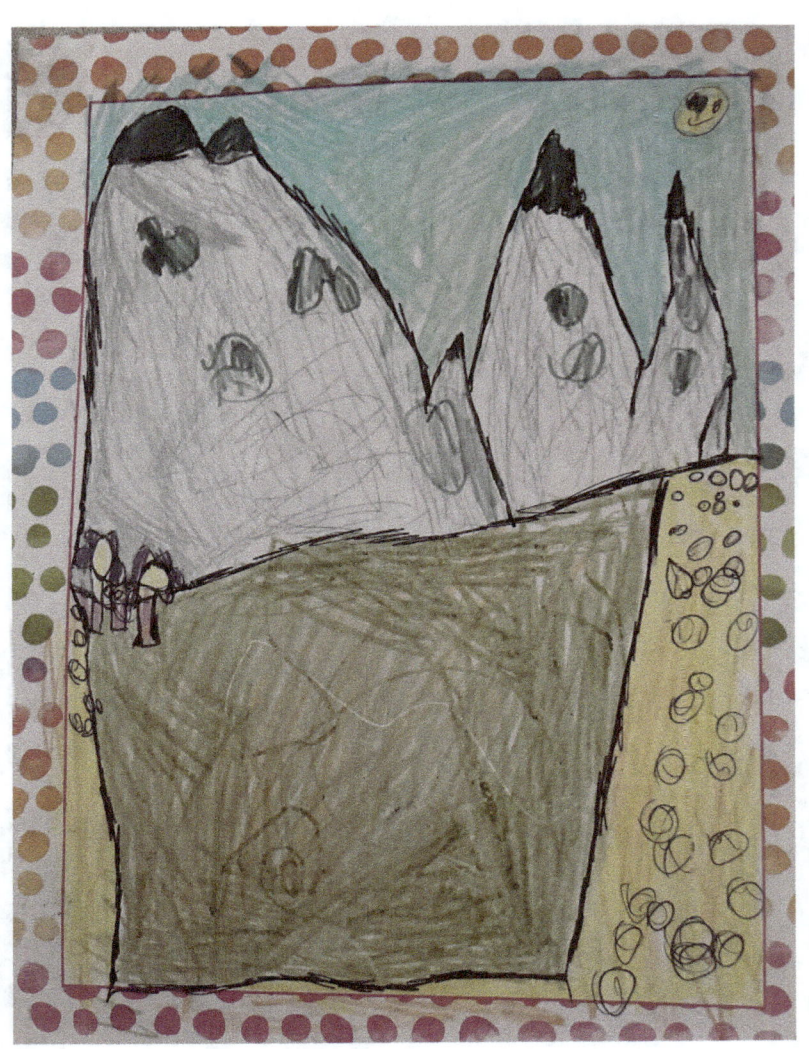

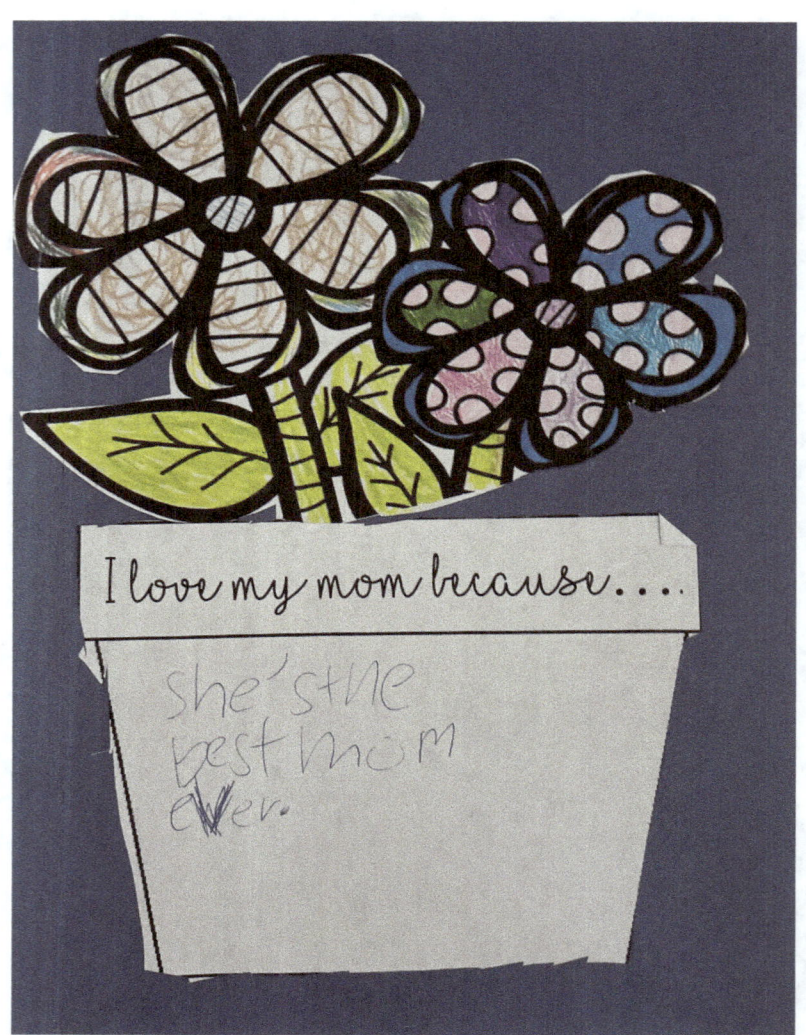

I love my mom because....

she's the best mom ever.

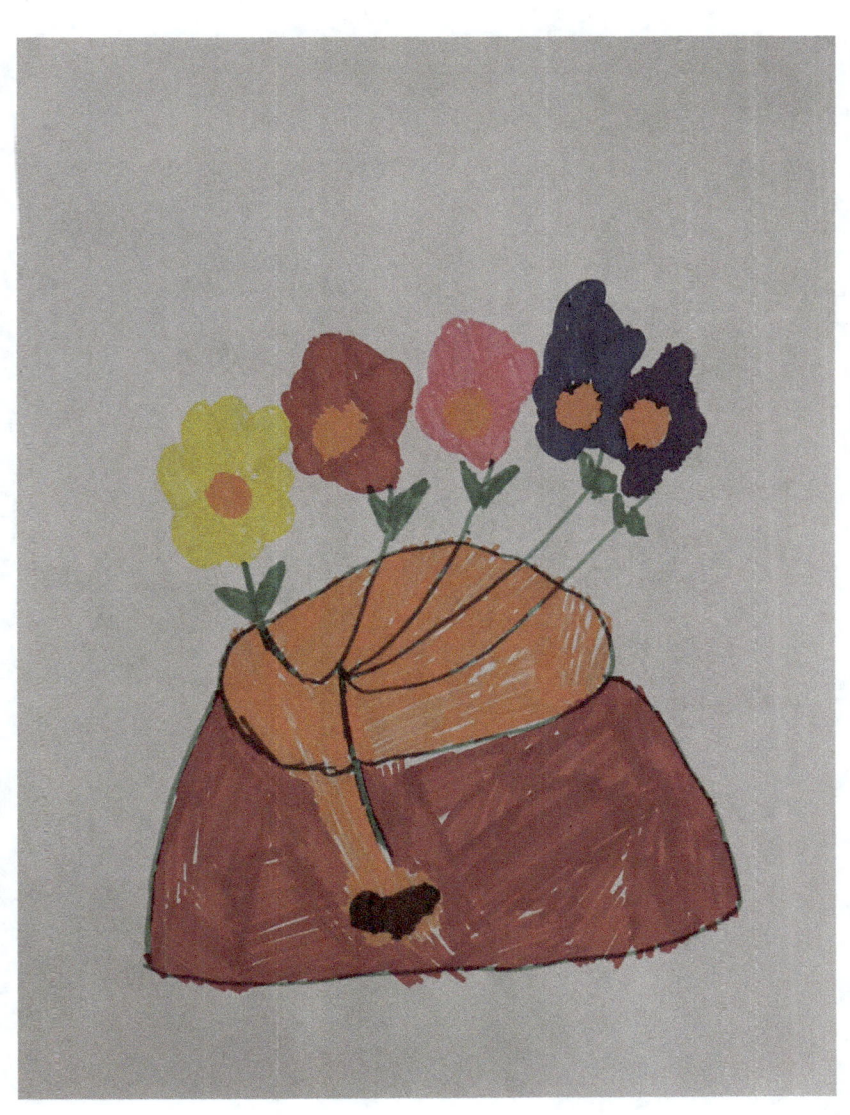

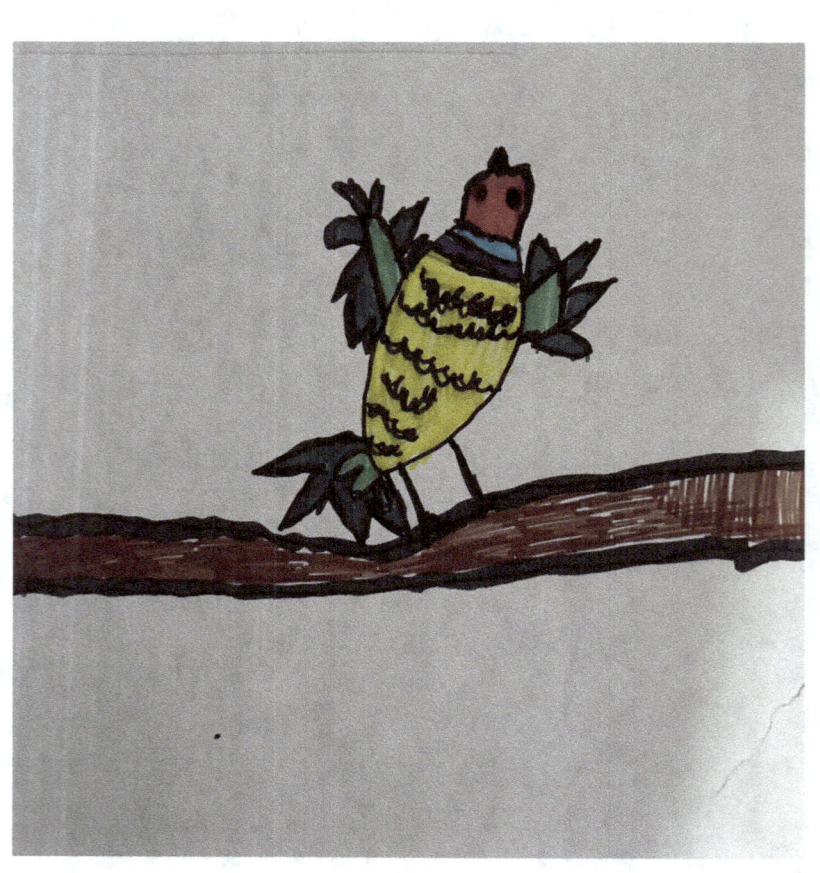

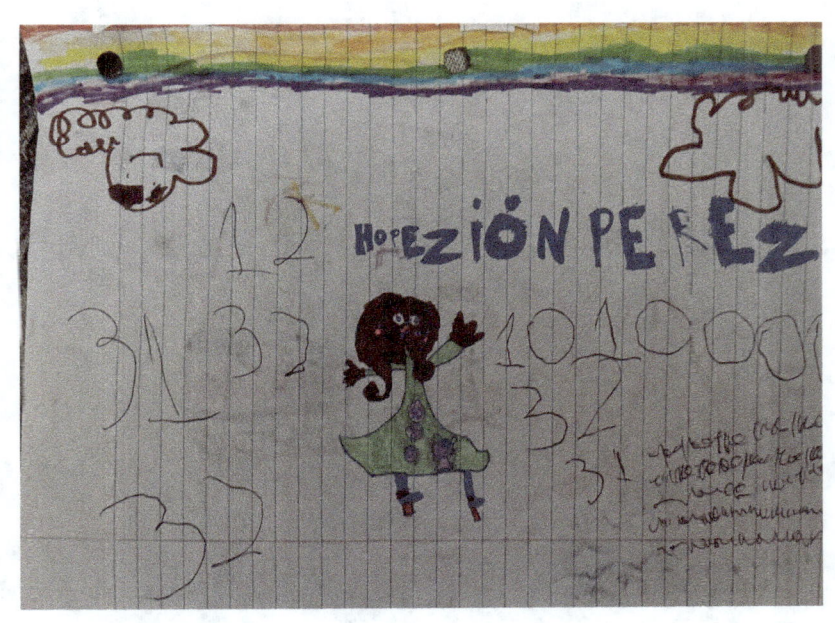

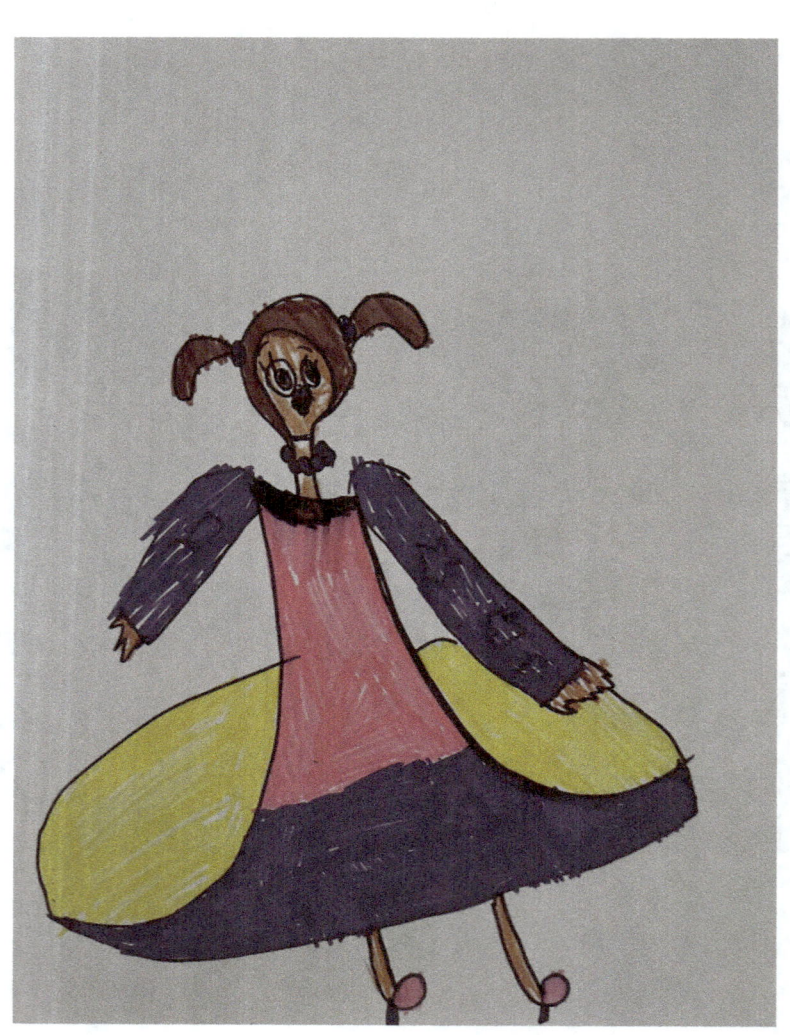

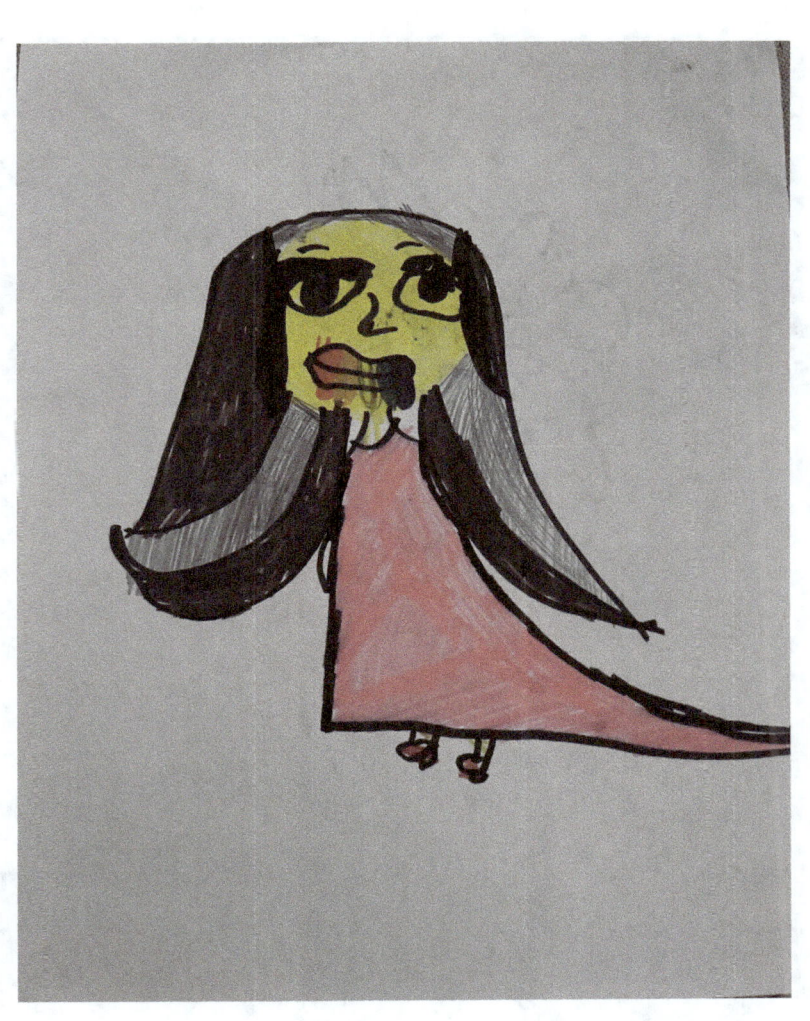

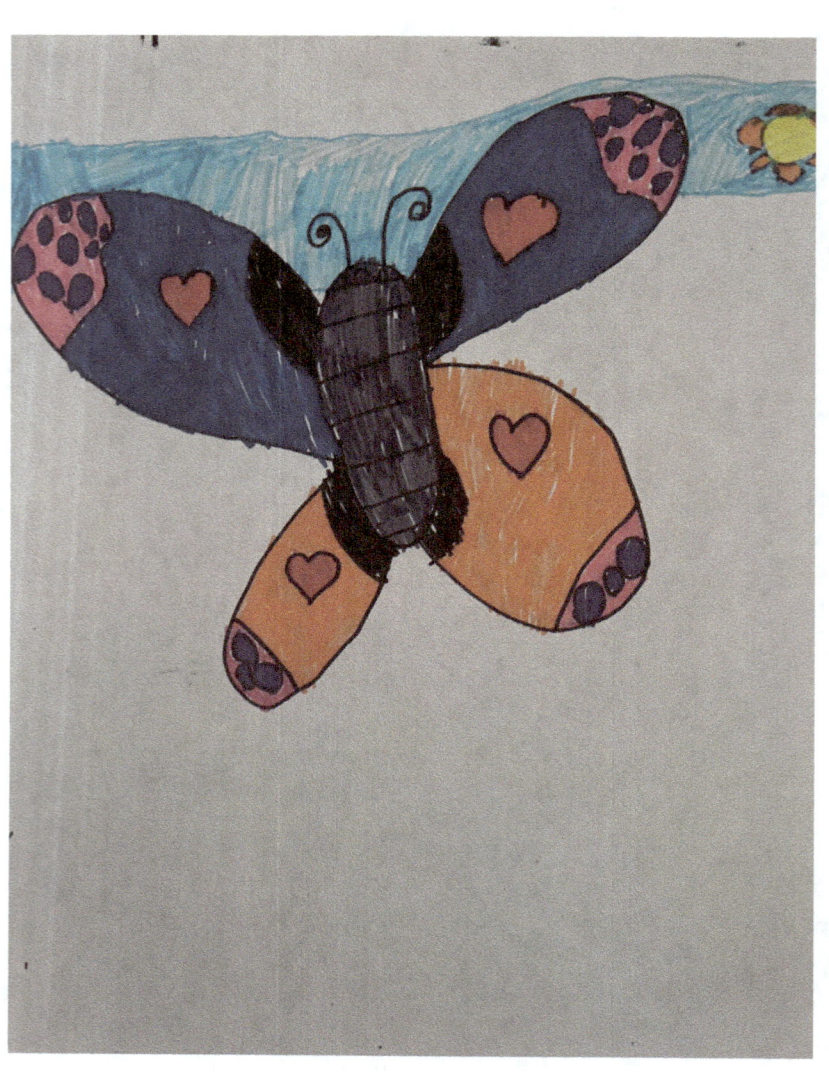

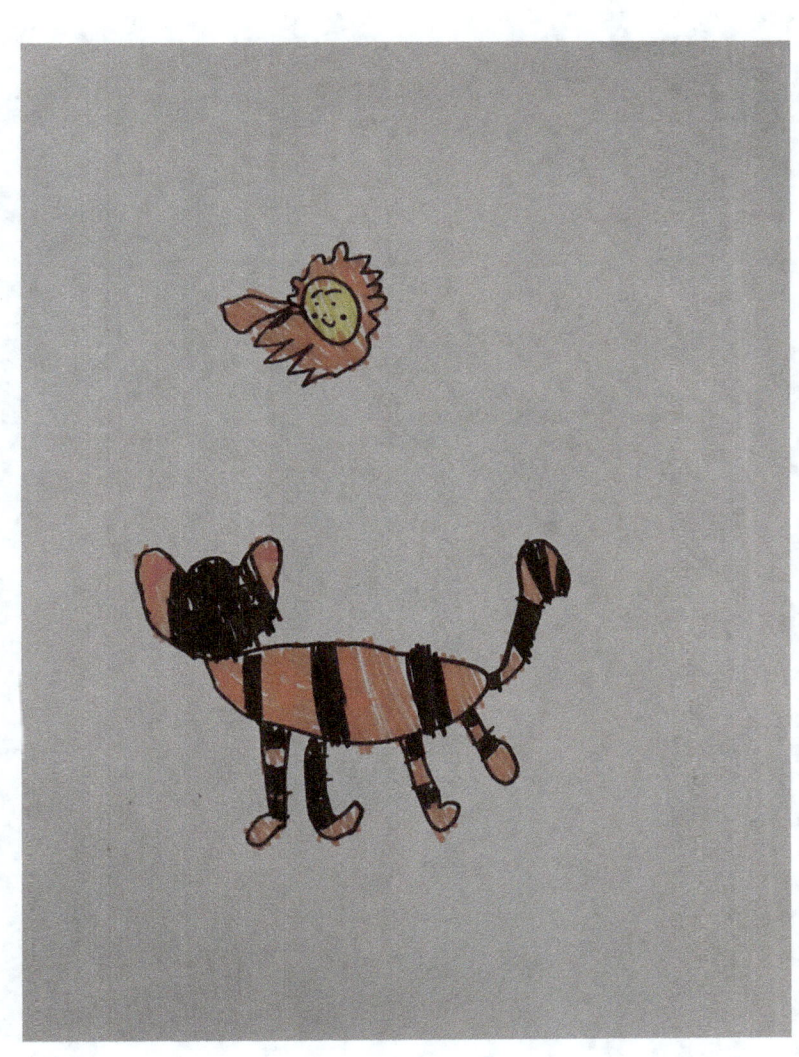

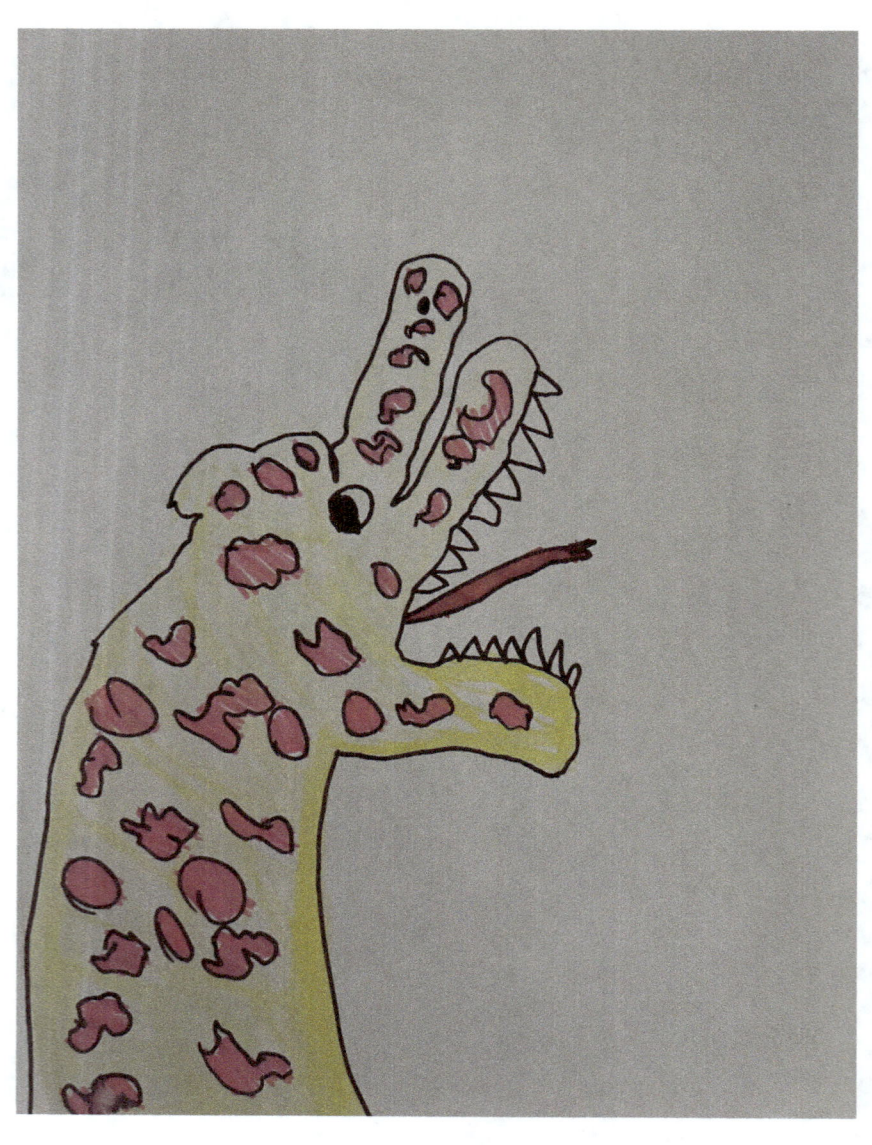

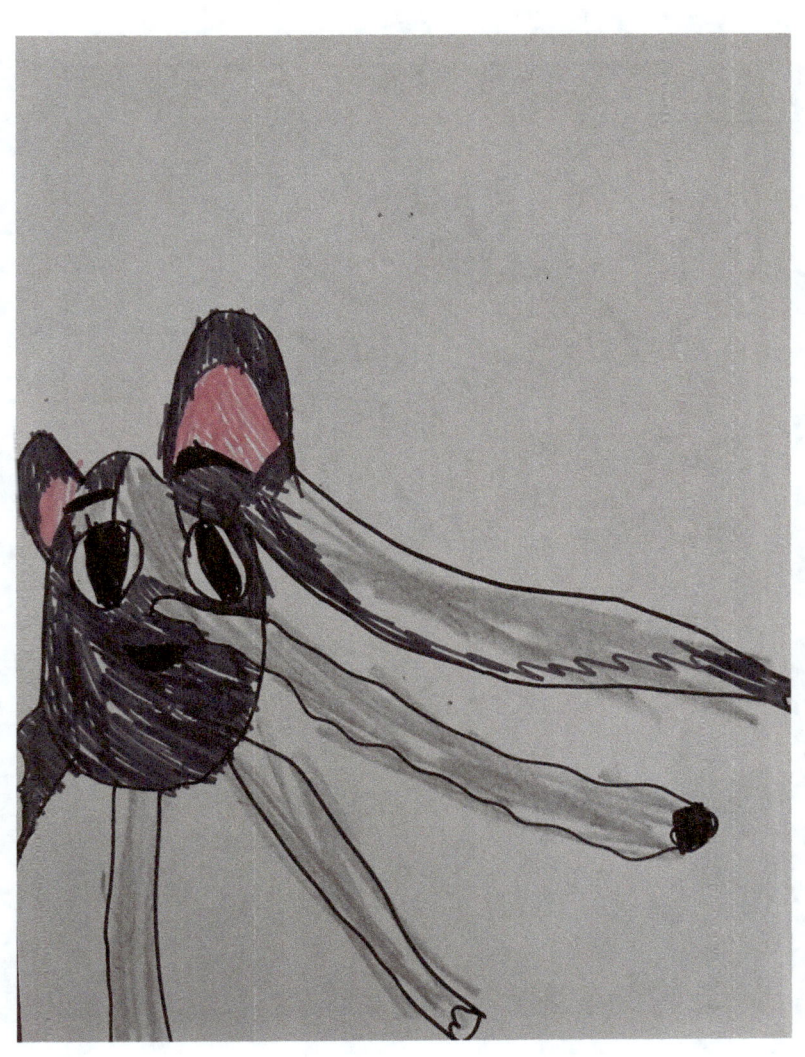

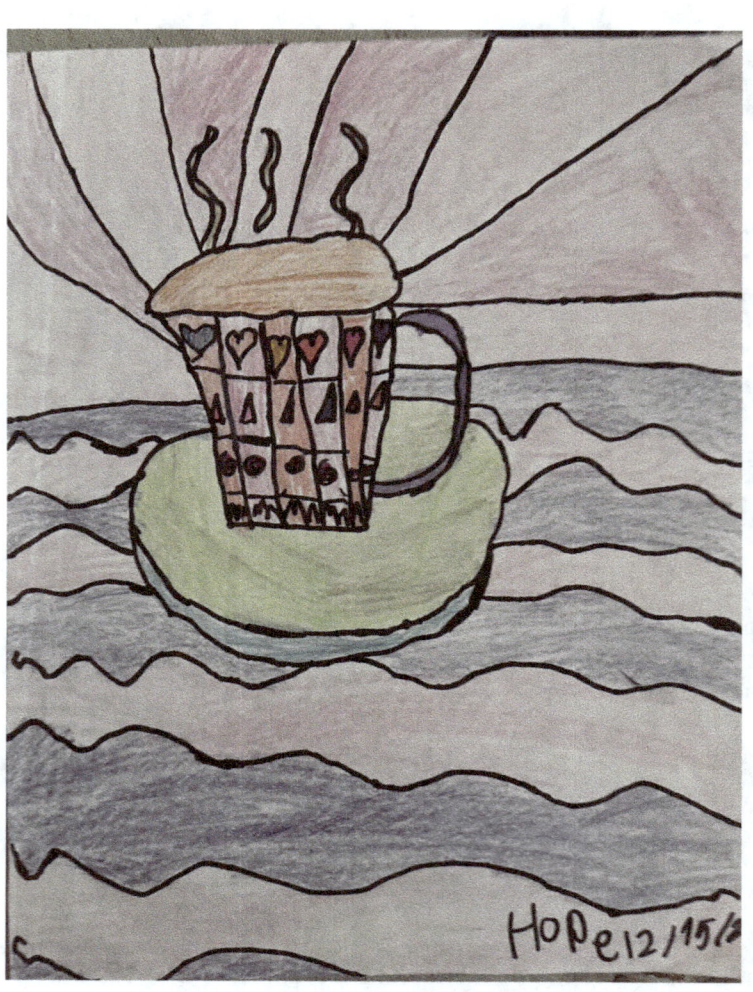

Hope 12/15/2

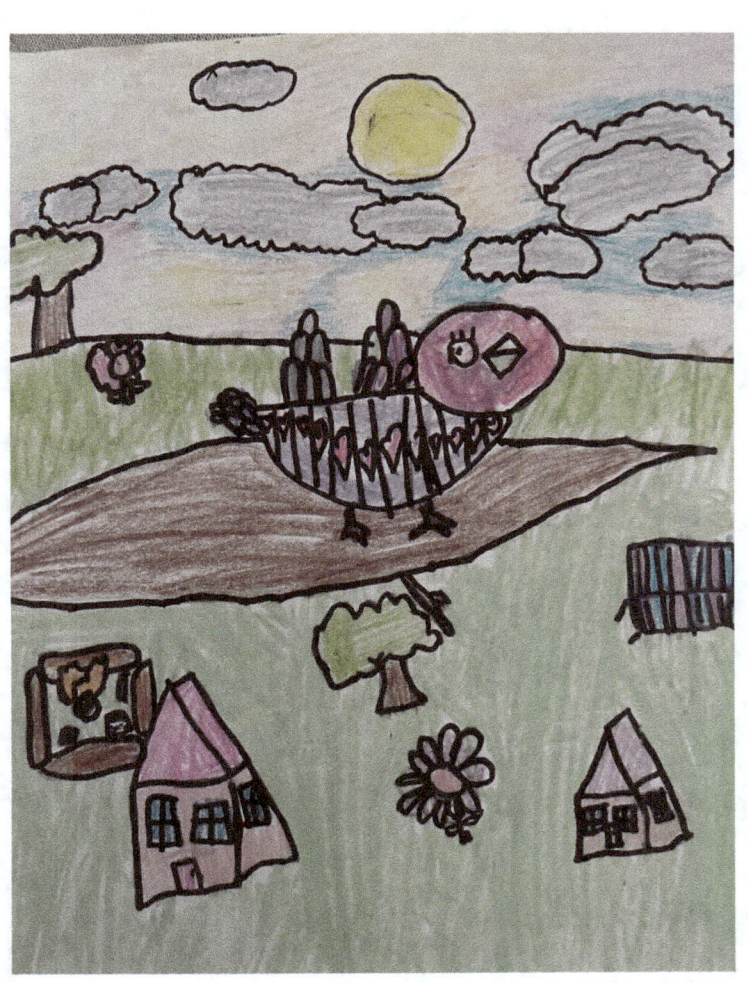

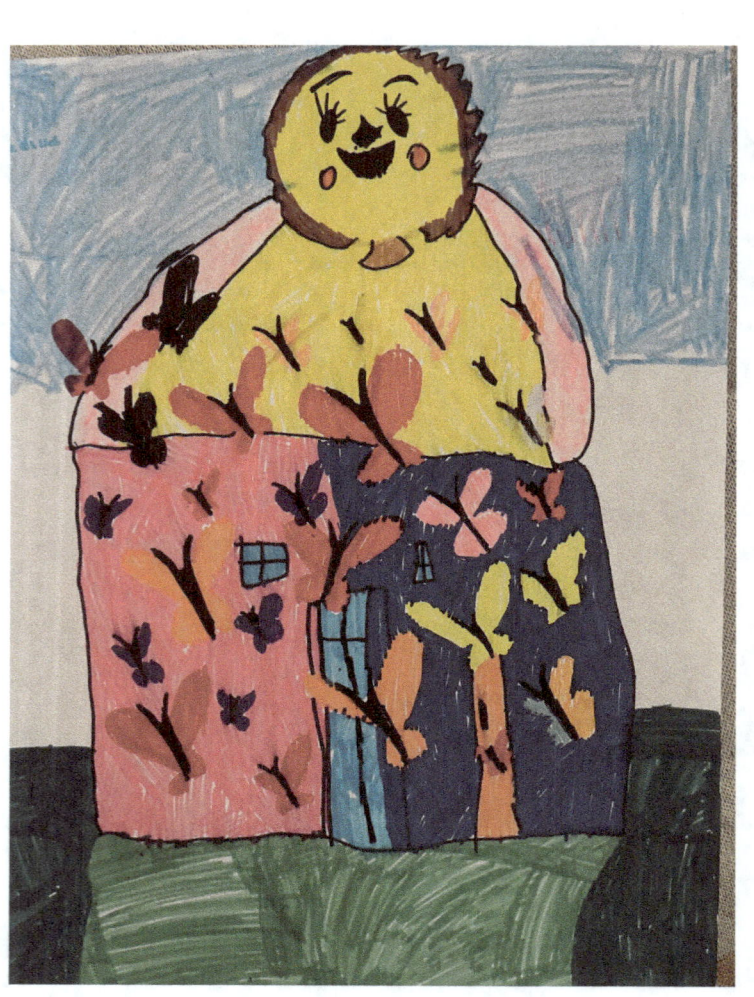

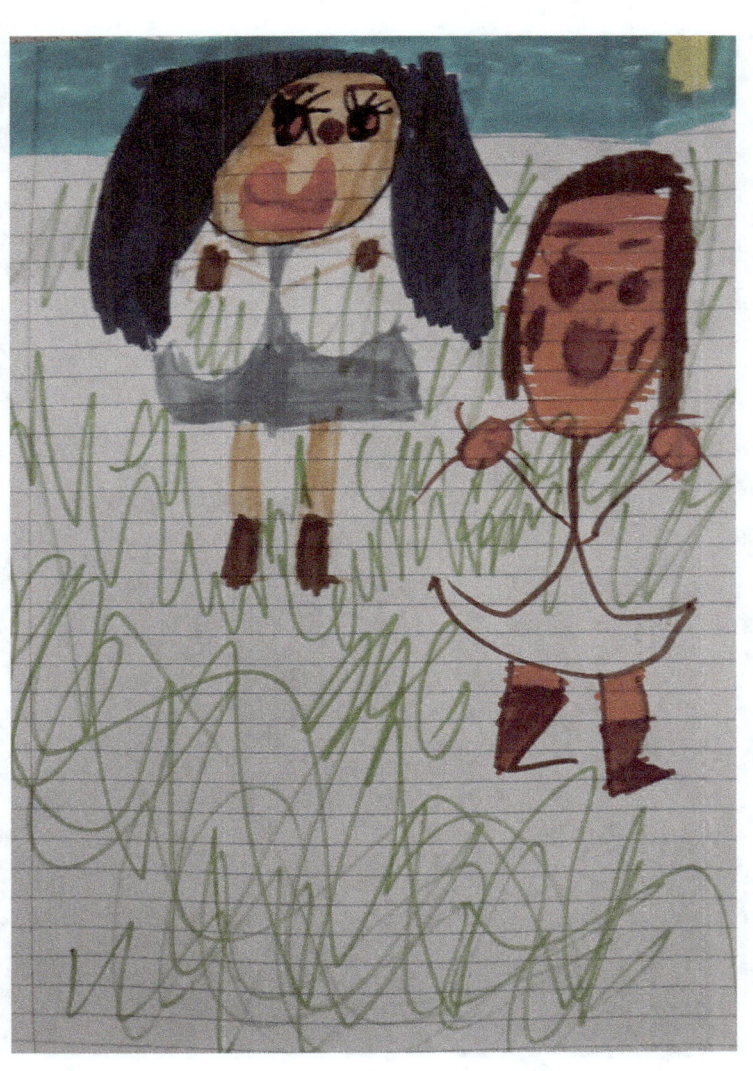

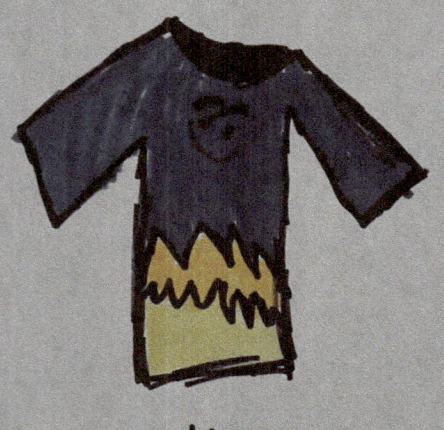

DADDY

HOPE ZION PEREZ

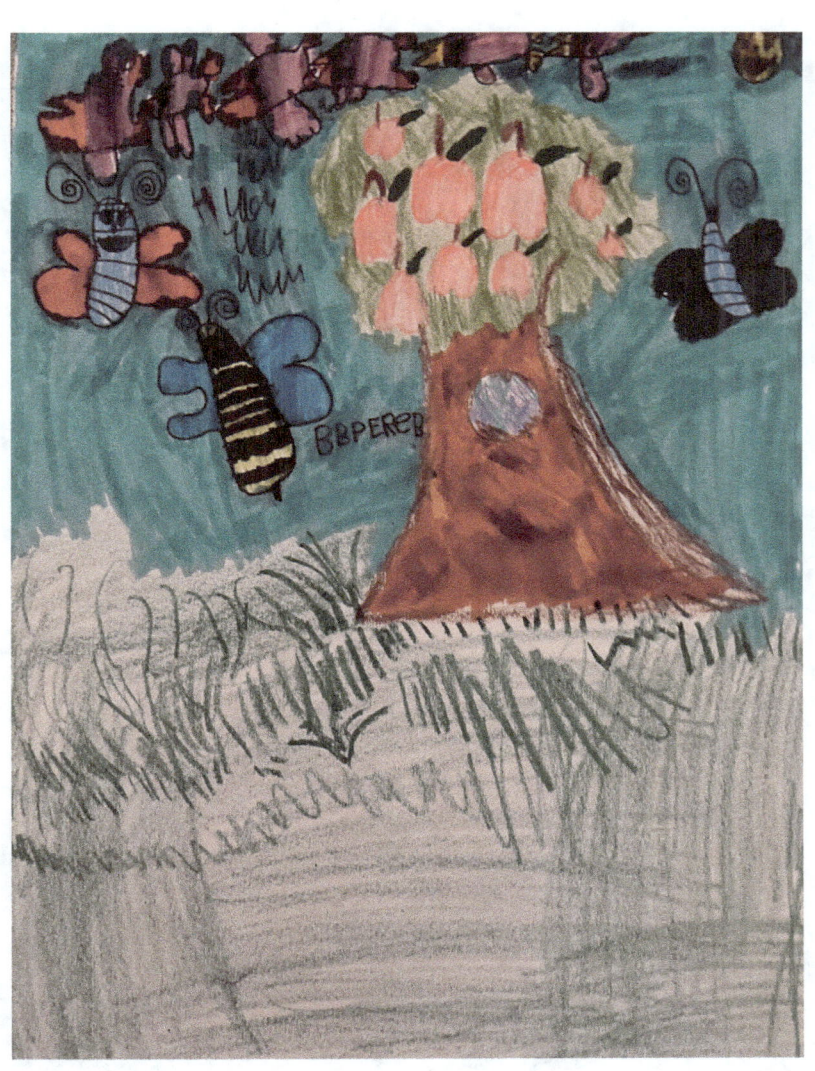

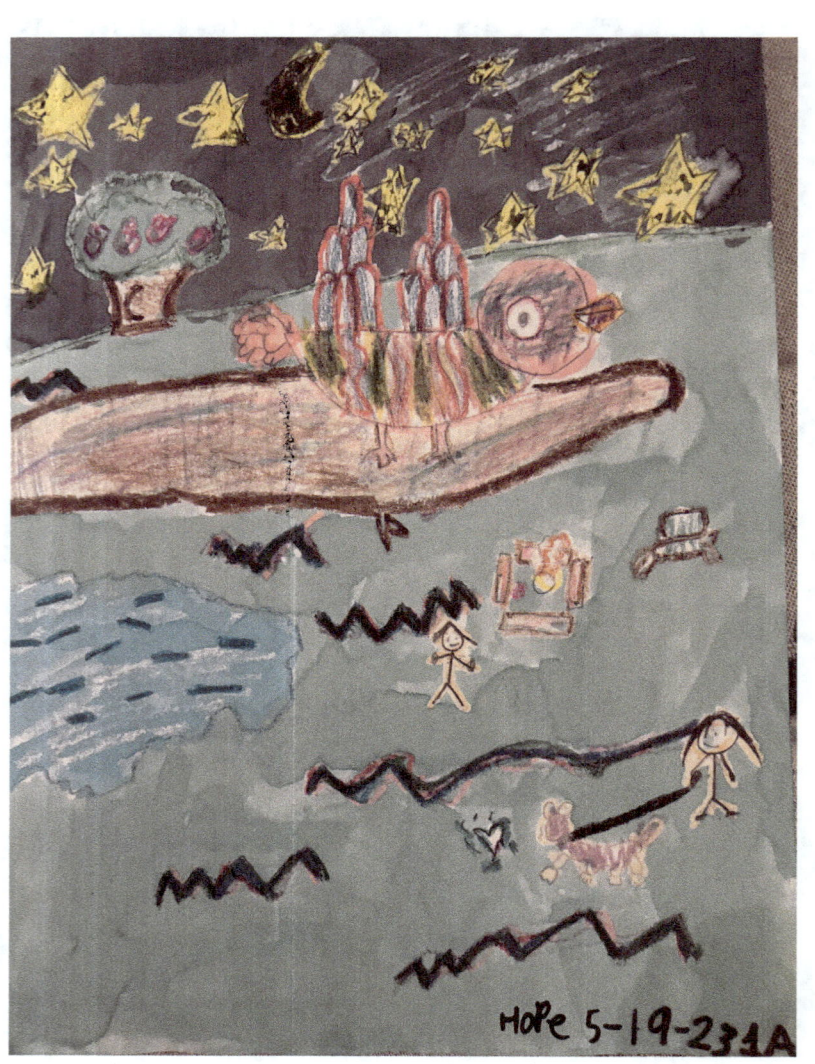

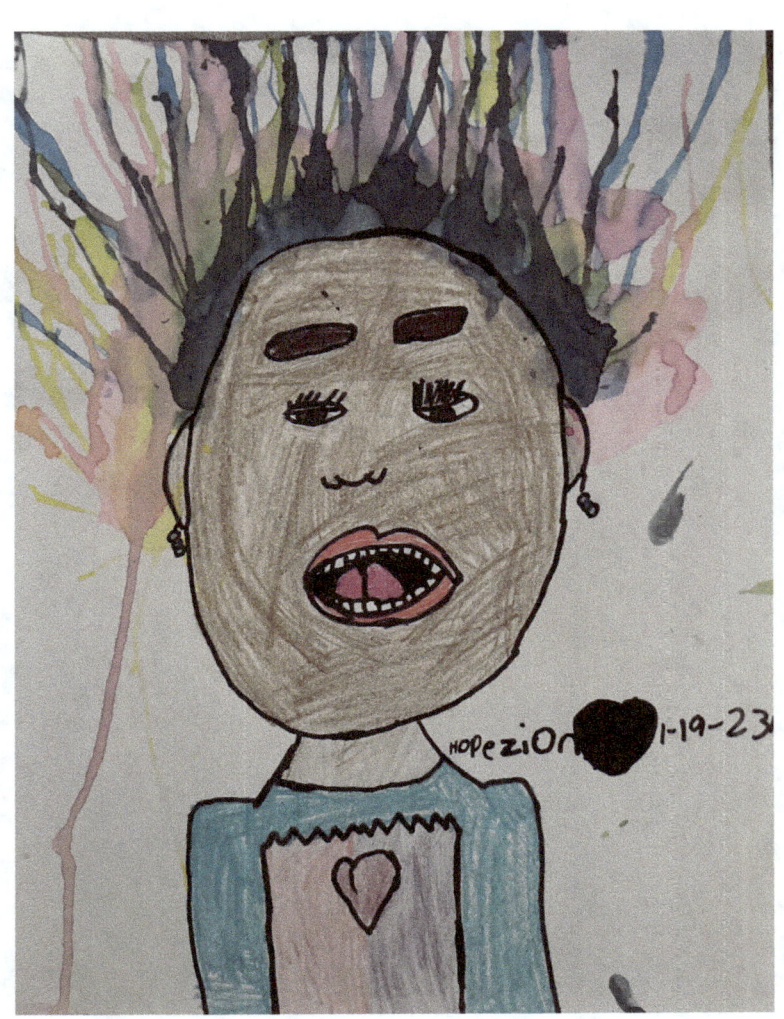

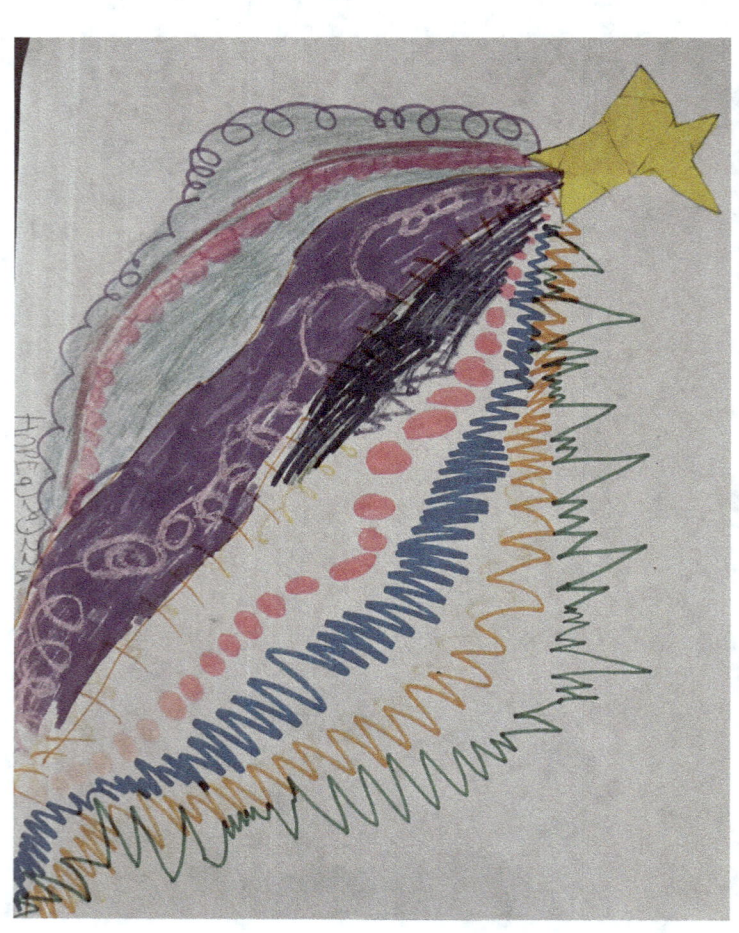

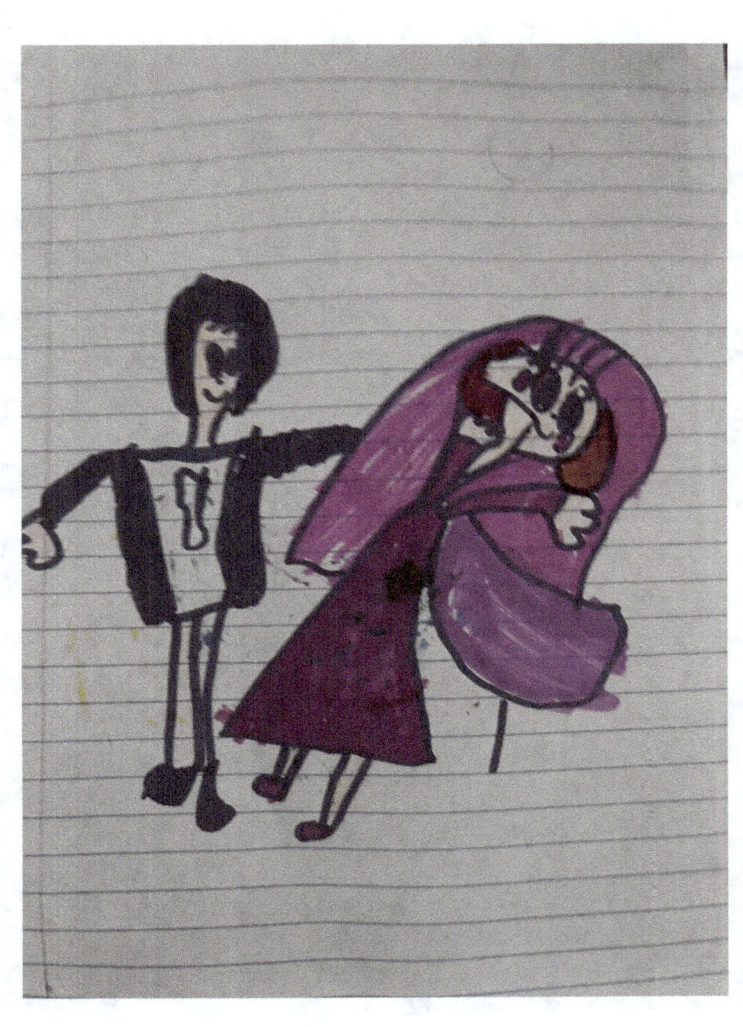

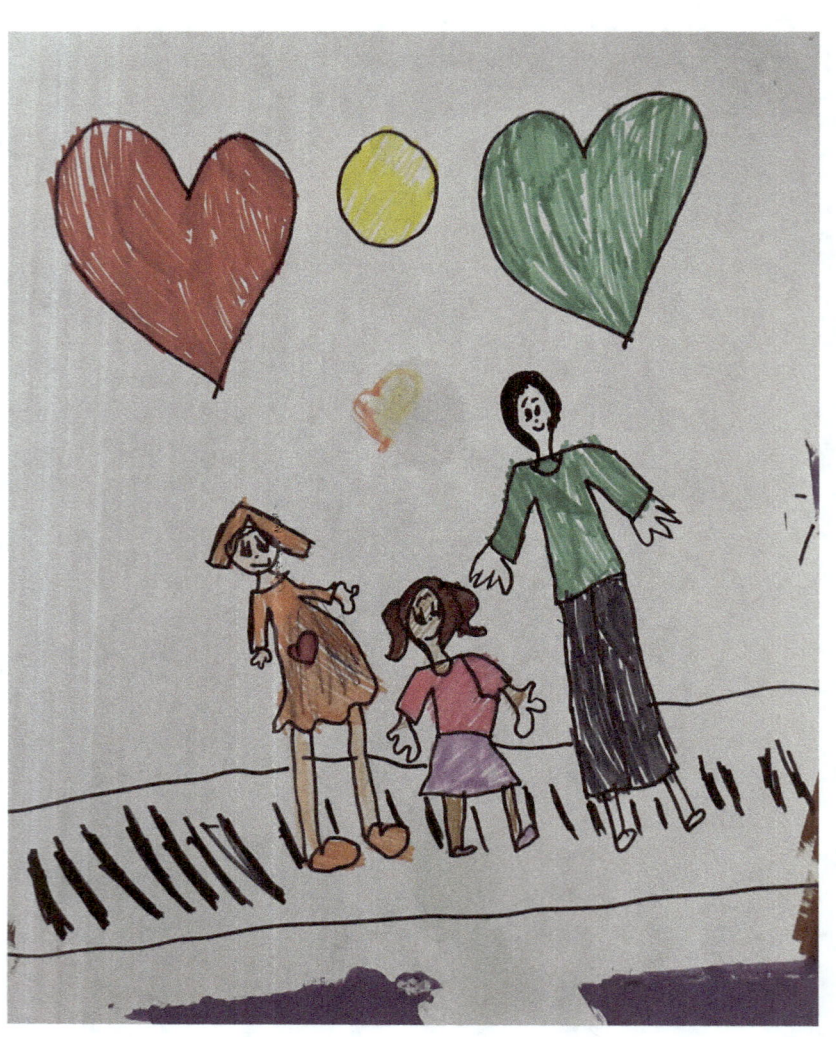

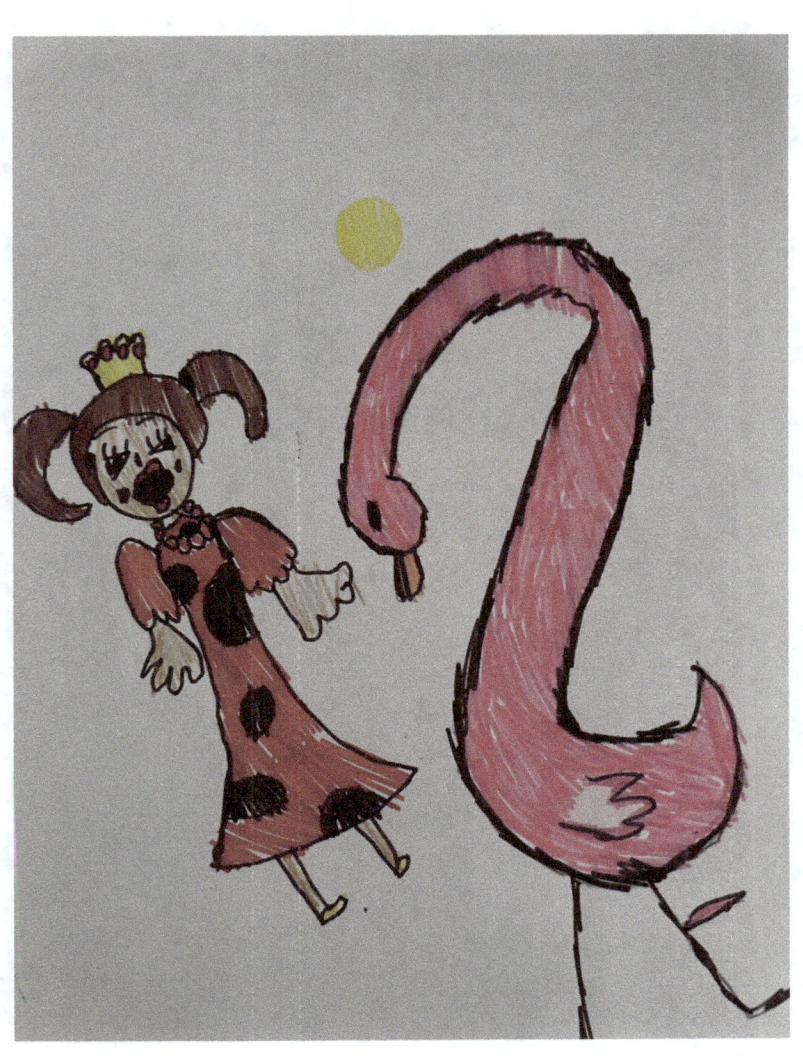

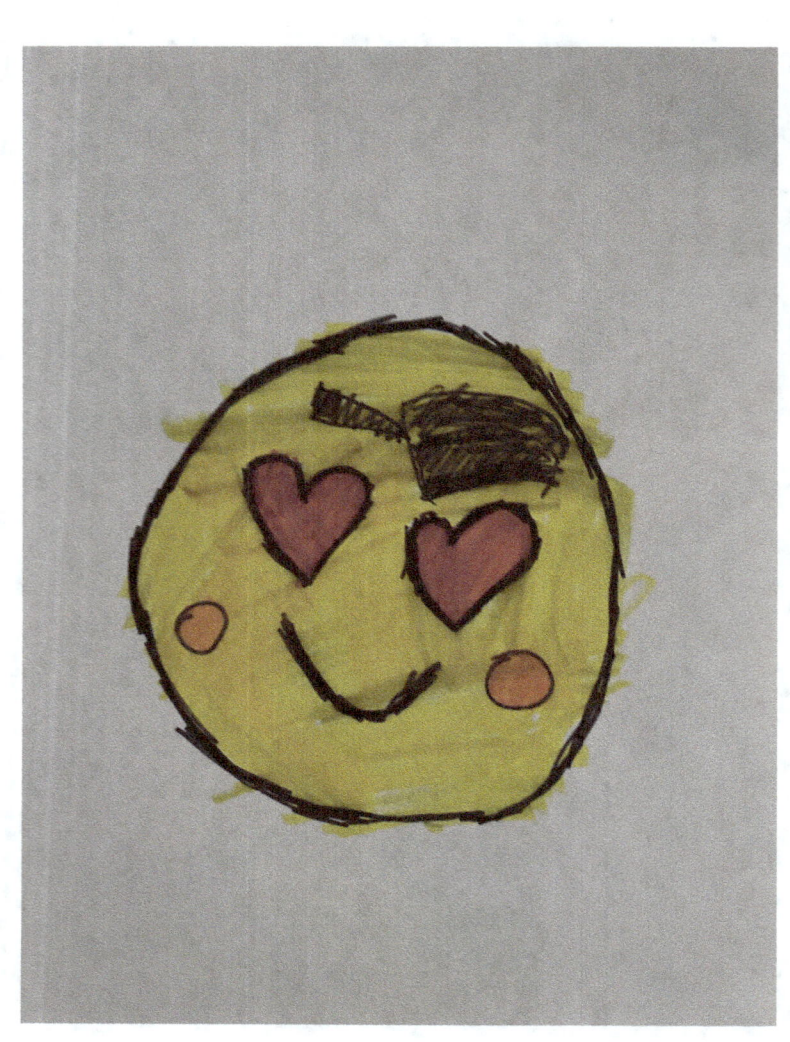

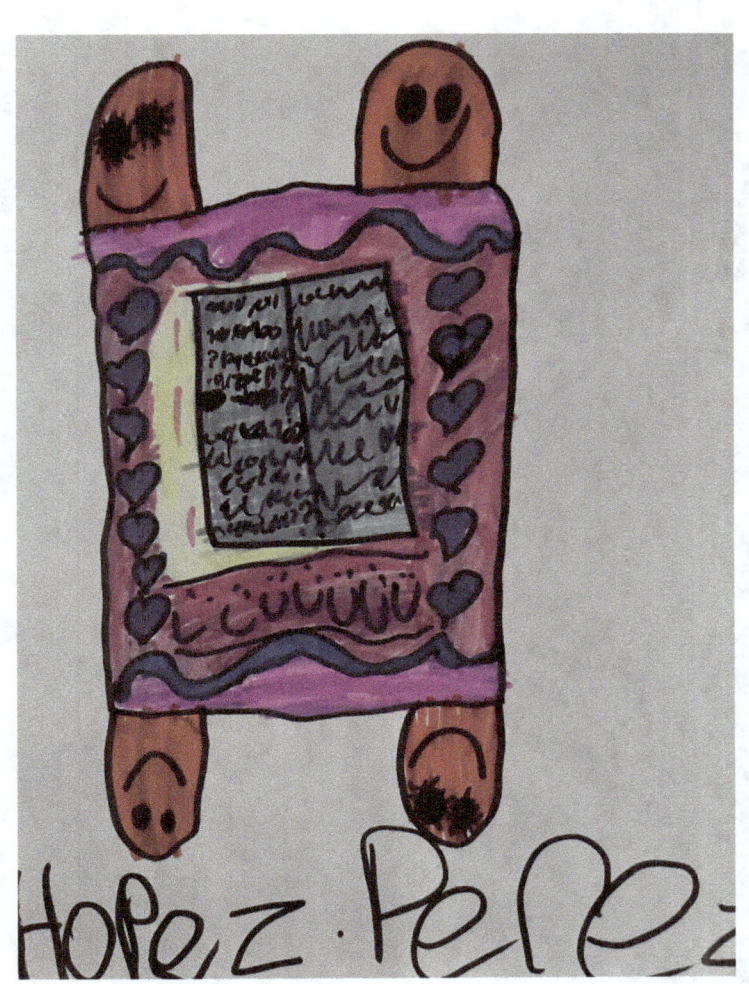

Hopez . Pepez

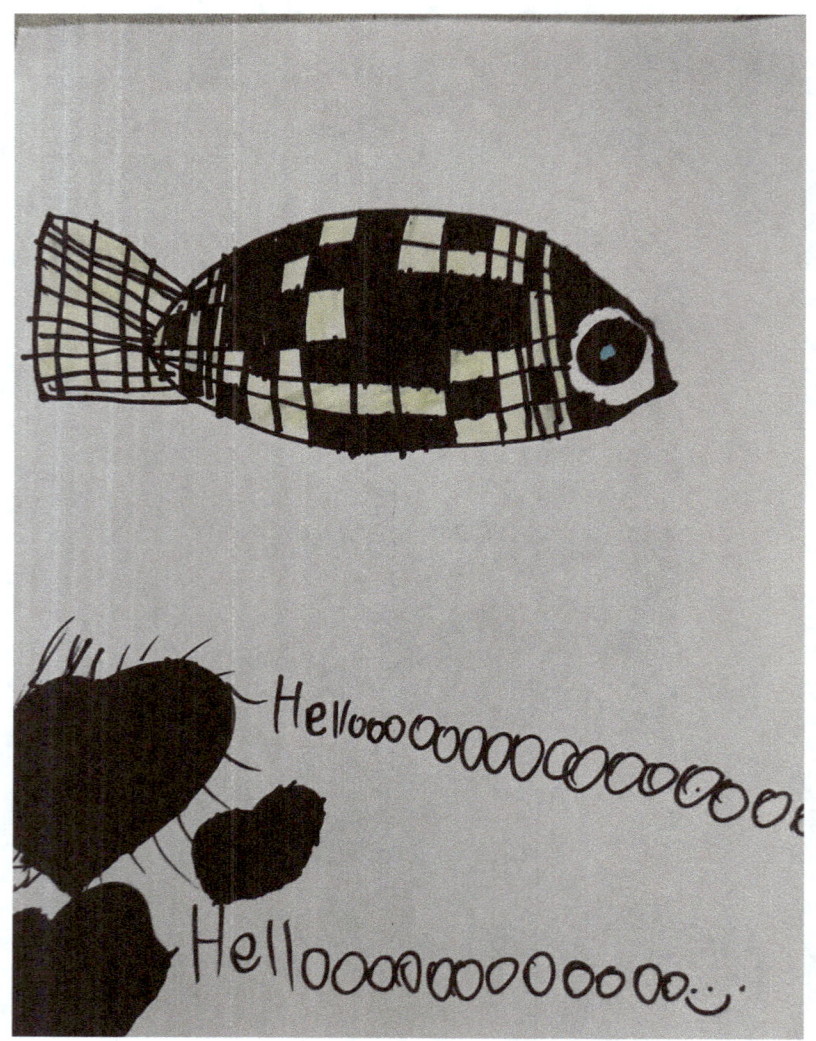

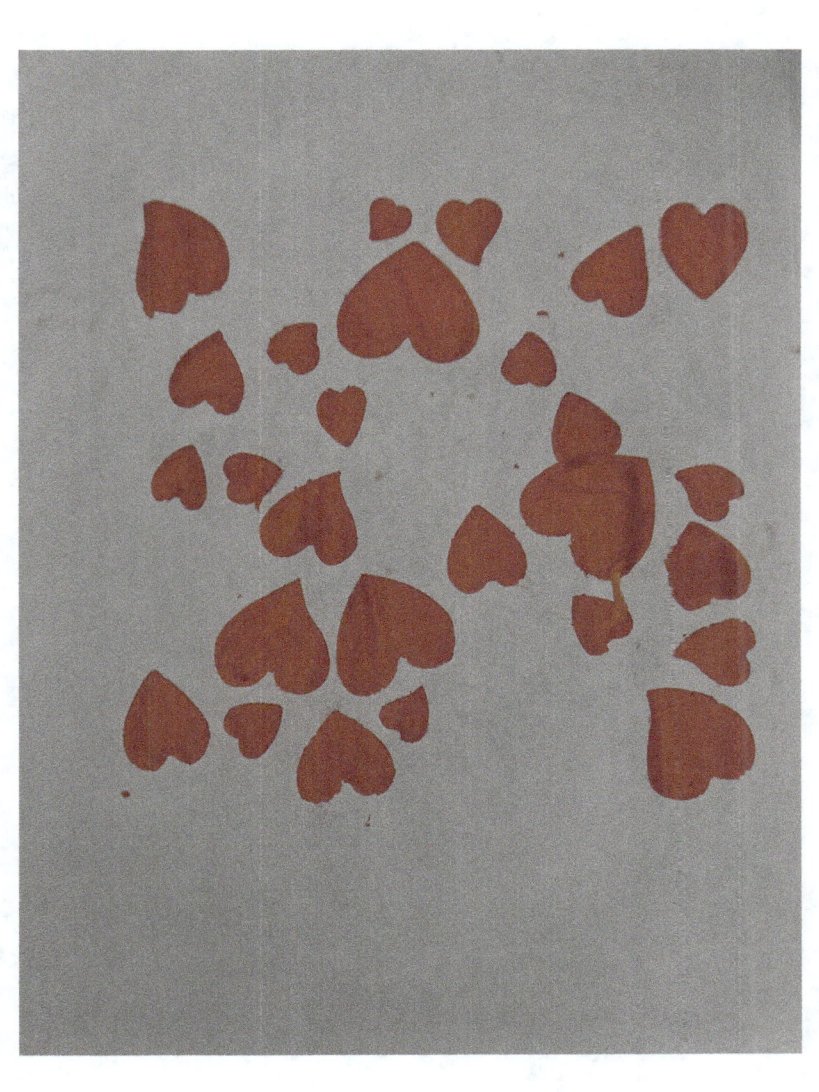

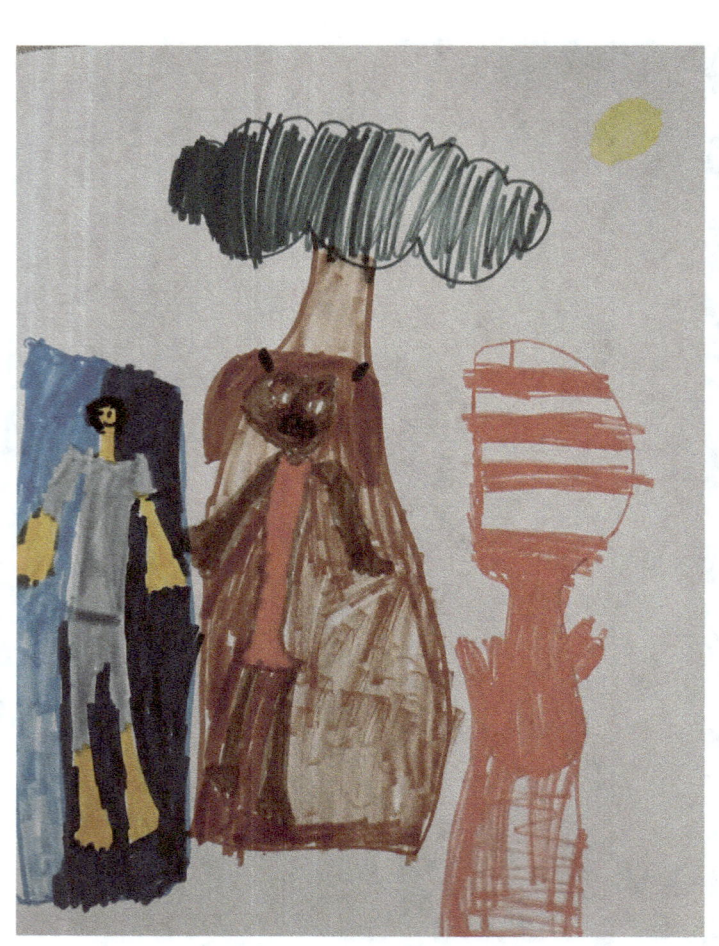

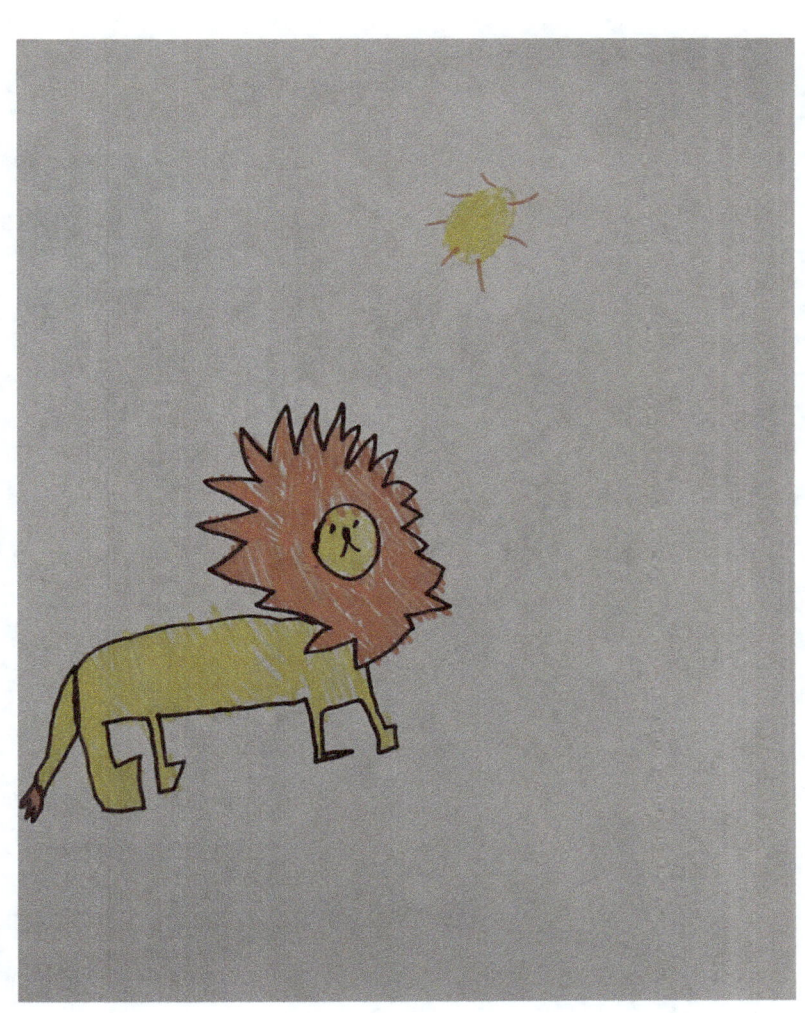

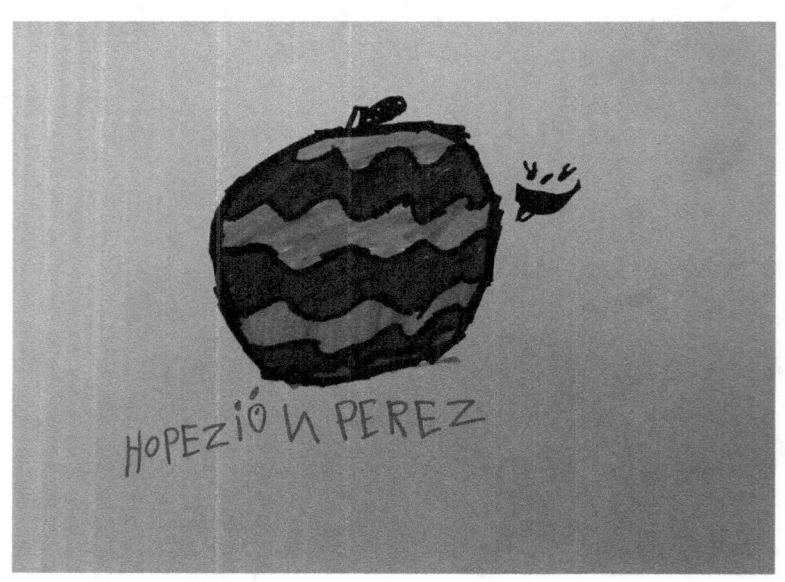

HOPEZIÓN PEREZ

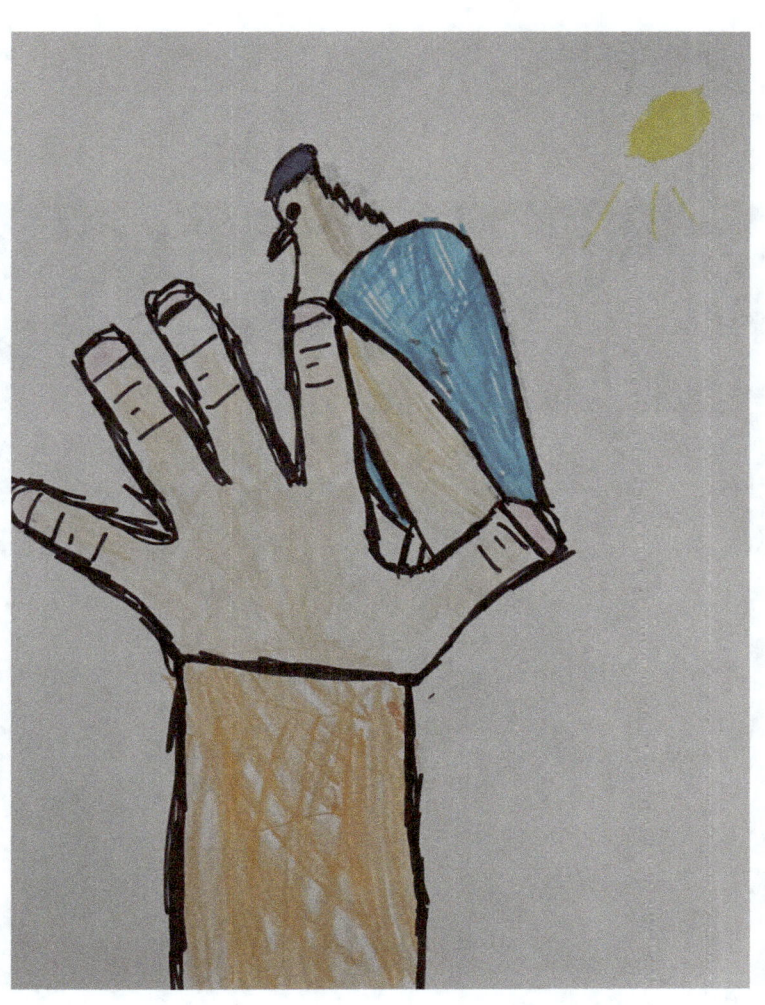

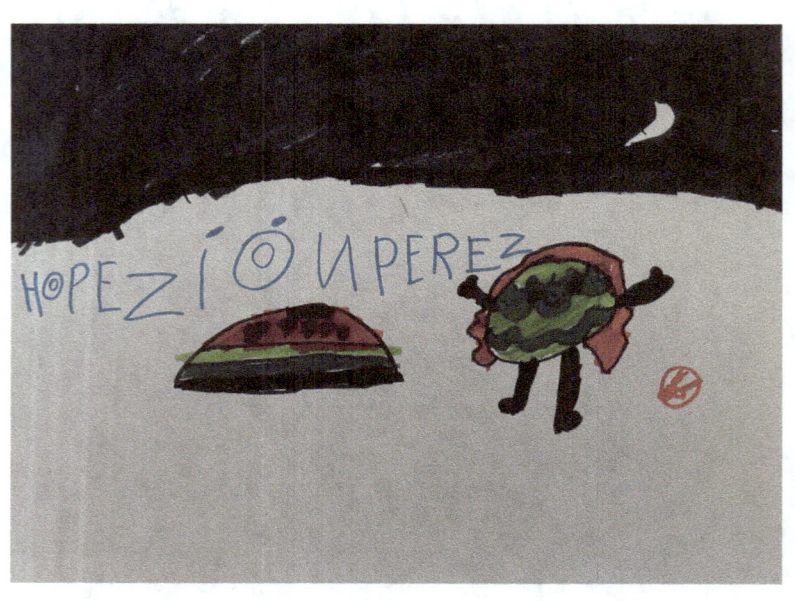

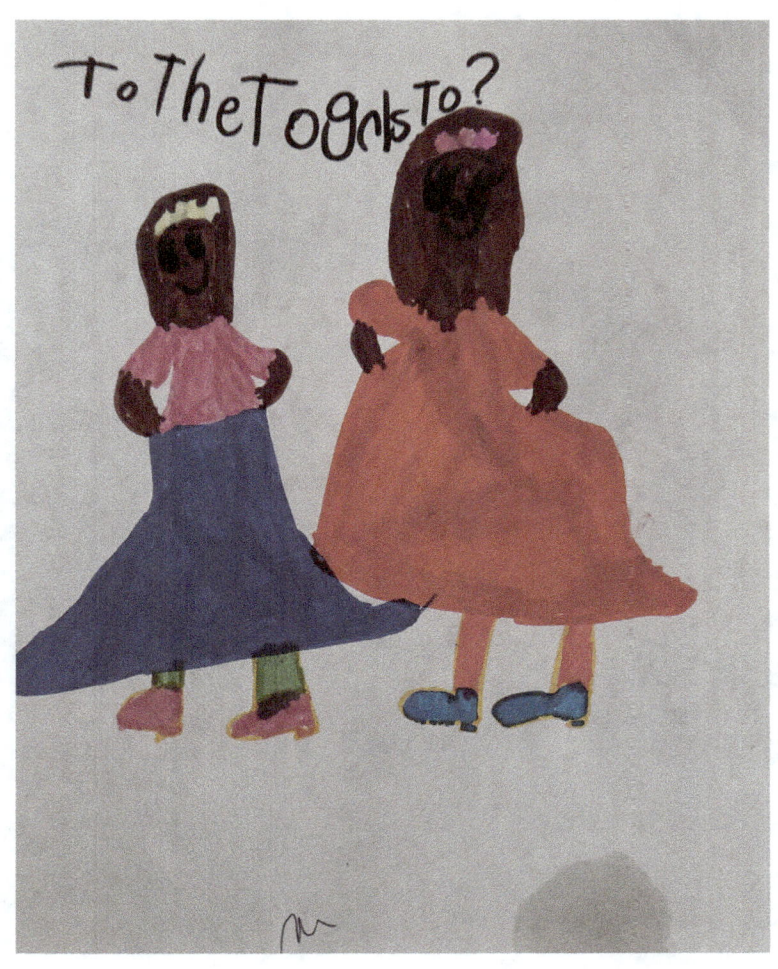

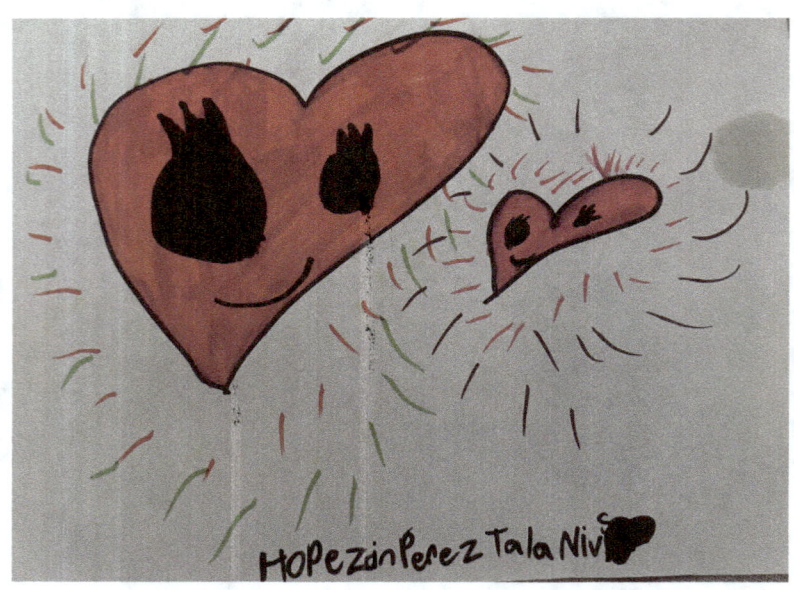

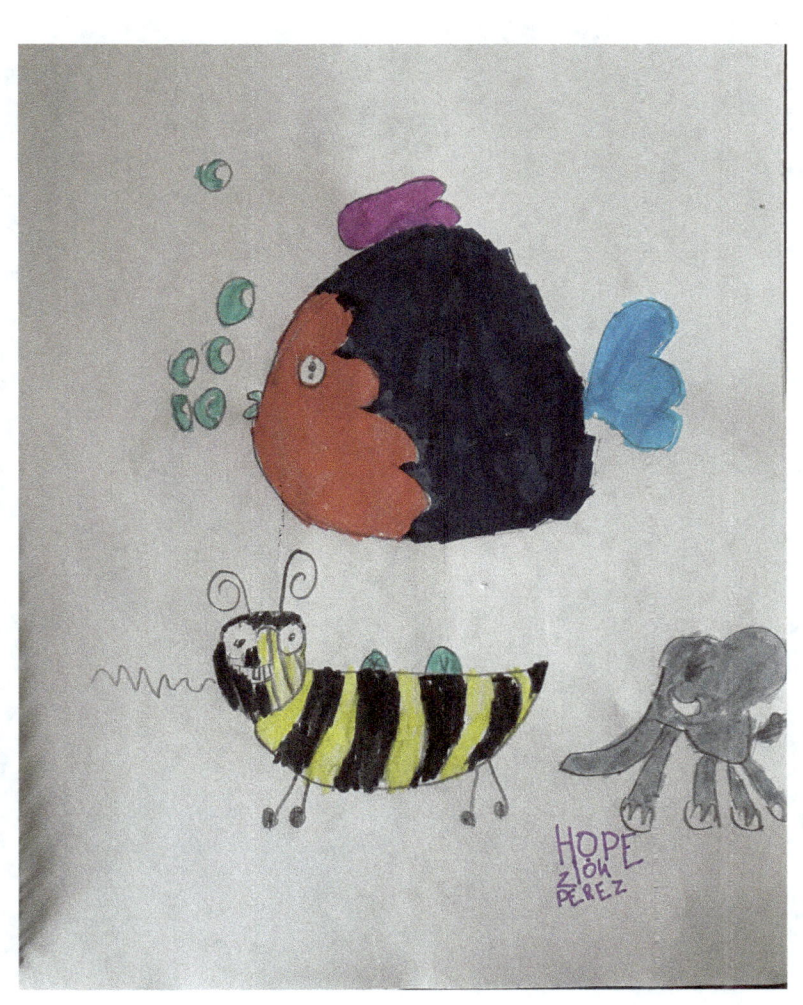

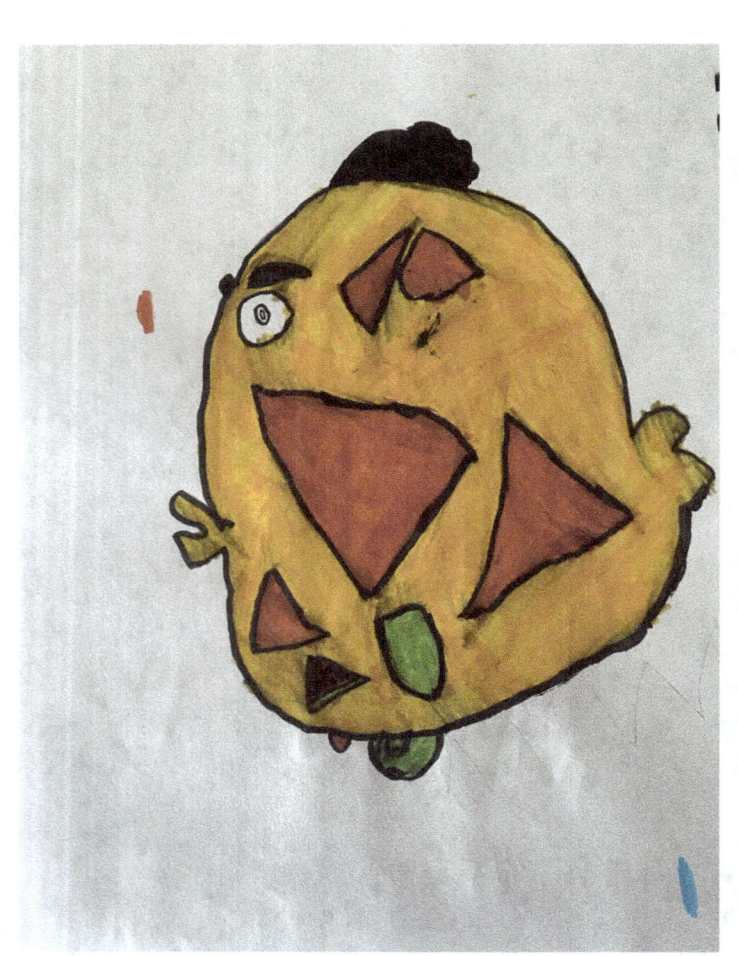

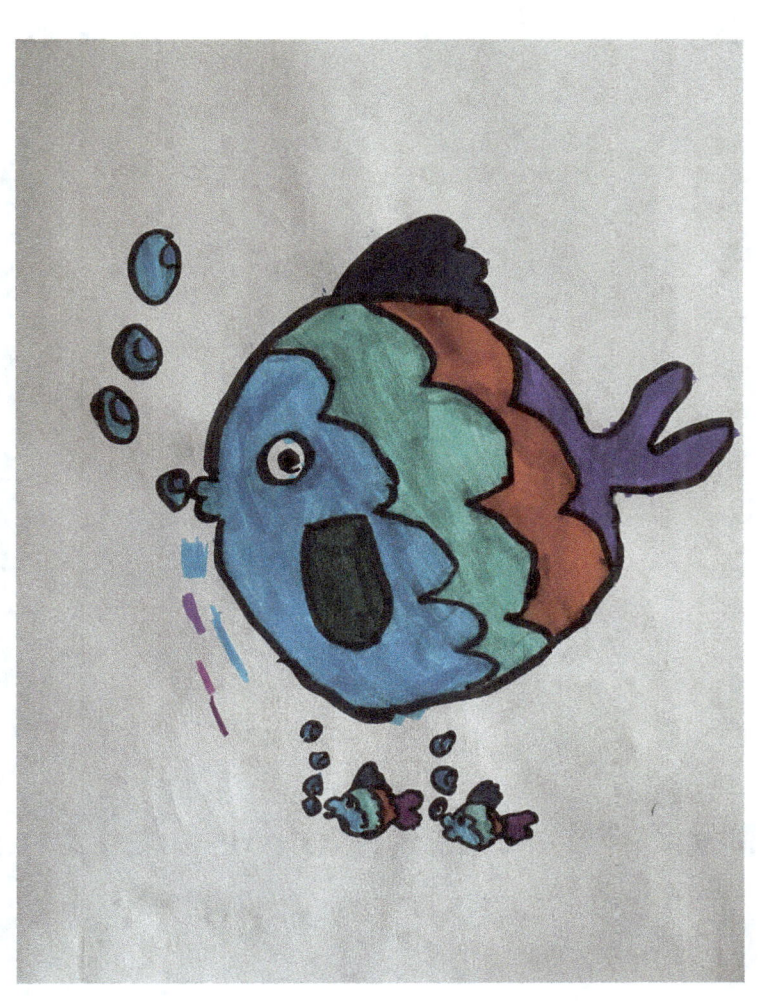

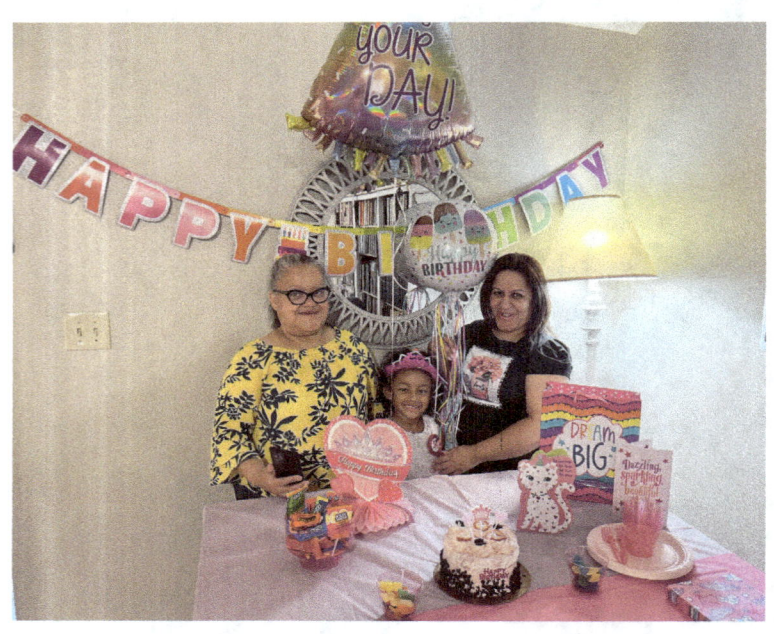

My 7th Birthday and my Grandma Aida came for my birthday!

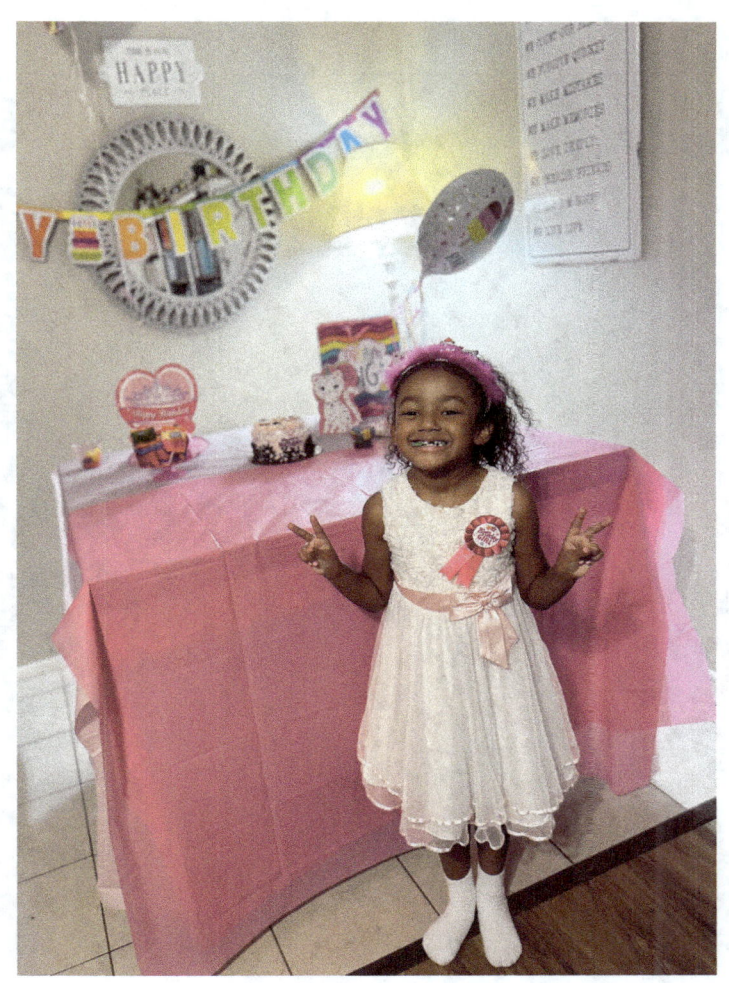

I pray and hope you enjoyed my artwork!

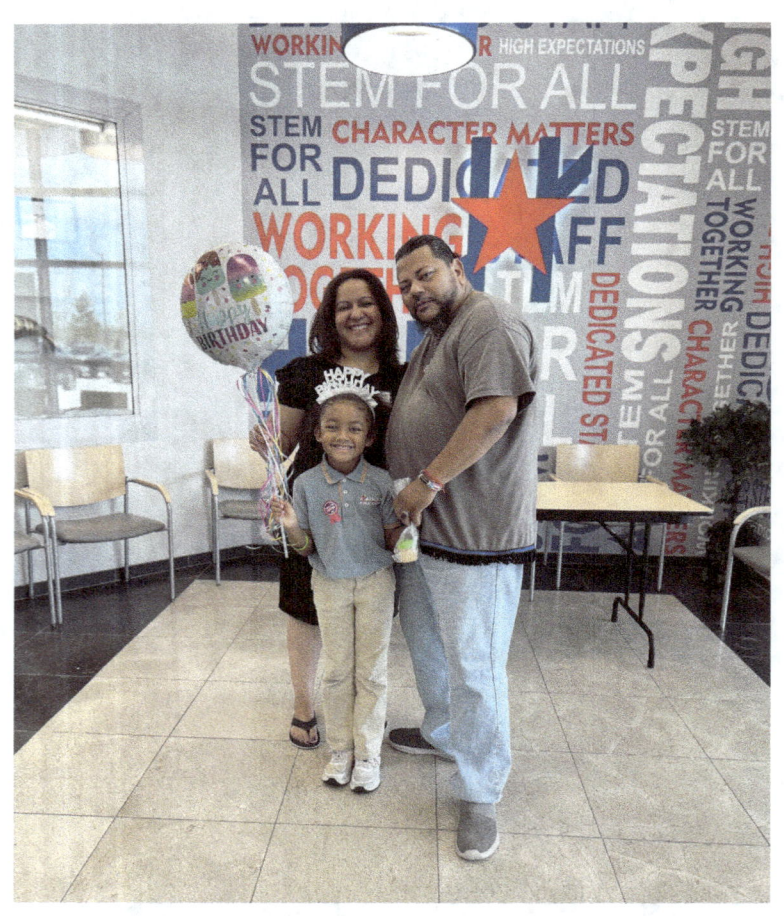

**My Mommy and Daddy
surprised me for my birthday at
school. I had so much fun!**

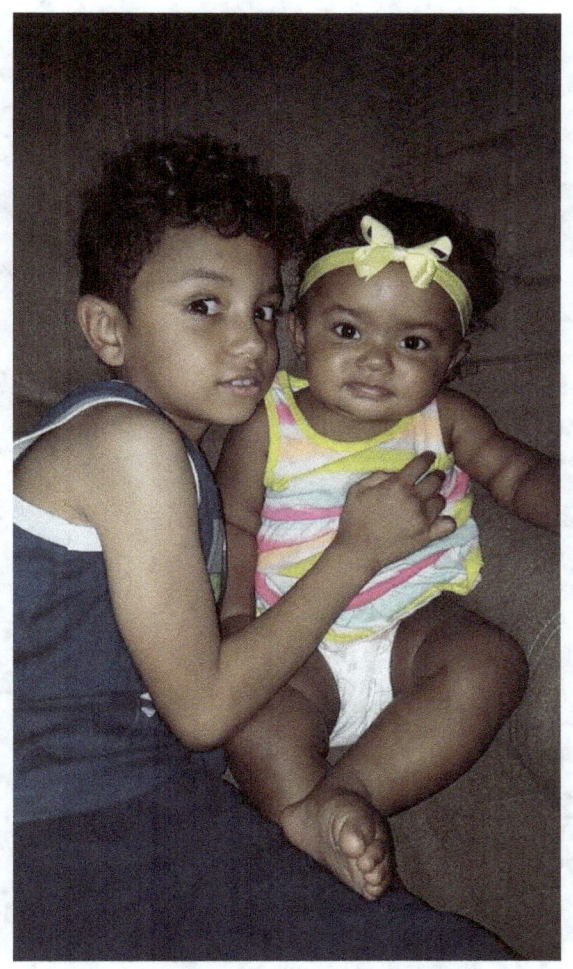

My brother Kaleb always taking
care of me since I was a baby.

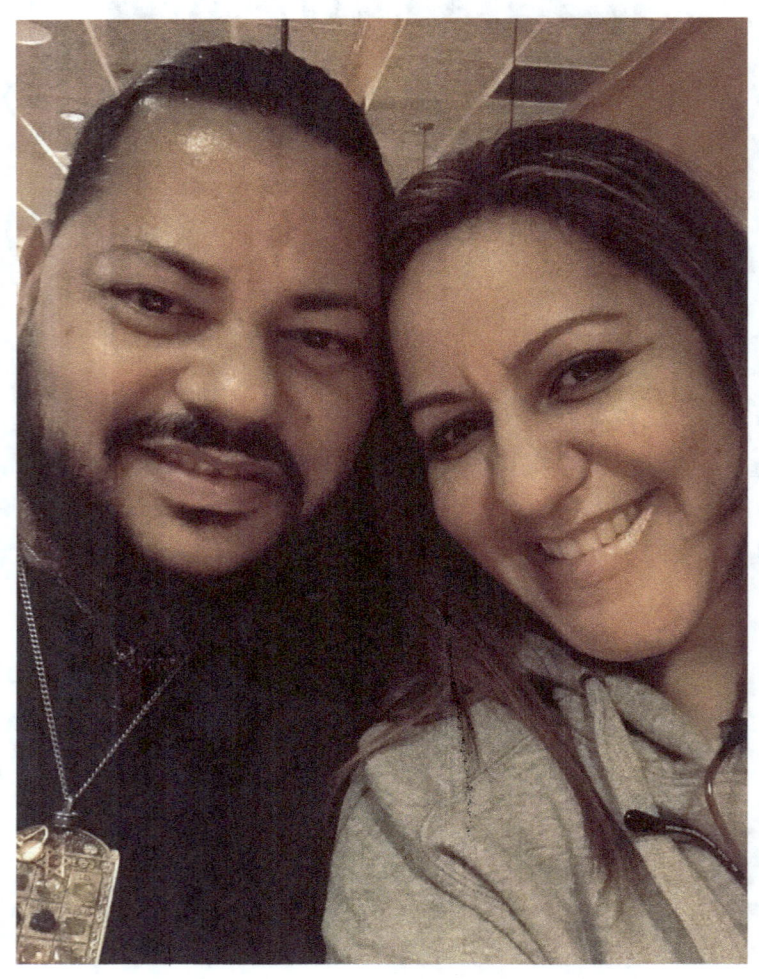

My daddy and Mommy

I hope you enjoyed my artwork!
Much Love Hope Zion